Author Day Adventures

Bringing Literacy to Life with an Author Visit

Helen Foster James

THE SCARECROW PRESS, INC.

Lanham, Maryland, and Oxford

2003

SCARECROW PRESS, INC.

Published in the United States of America
by Scarecrow Press, Inc.
A Member of the Rowman & Littlefield Publishing Group
4720 Boston Way, Lanham, Maryland 20706
www.scarecrowpress.com

PO Box 317
Oxford
OX2 9RU, UK

British Library Cataloguing in Publication Information Available

Library of Congress Cataloging-in-Publication Data

James, Helen Foster.
    Author day adventures : bringing literacy to life with an author
visit / Helen Foster James.
        p. cm.
    Includes bibliographical references and index.
    ISBN 0-8108-4370-6 (alk. paper)
    1. School libraries—Activity programs. 2. Children—Books and
reading. 3. Language arts. 4. Reading promotion. I. Title.
Z675.S3J26 2003
027.8—dc21

                                            2002010773

♾™ The paper used in this publication meets the minimum requirements of
American National Standard for Information Sciences—Permanence of Paper for
Printed Library Materials, ANSI/NISO Z39.48-1992.
Manufactured in the United States of America.

Contents

Drawing by M. Sarah Klise.

Acknowledgments

An enormous thank you to the wonderful authors and illustrators who graciously and generously donated material for me to share with you. I've been overwhelmed by their kindness and delighted by the original and personal items they contributed. You will find their names, suggestions, stories, and contact information sprinkled throughout this resource.

As always, I appreciate the support of my lunch group: Paul Brewer, Larry Dane Brimner, Jean Ferris, Kathleen Krull, and Pam Muñoz Ryan. These talented authors are always willing to help me brainstorm, to encourage me, and to offer fine suggestions. (By the way, we usually meet for lunch at Aesop's Tables, to keep a literary feel to the lunch!) She is well-known for her quirky and funny, right-on-target nonfiction books, and I wish her luck with her promising illustration career.

—Helen Foster James

Introduction

I will always treasure the memory of my first meeting with a children's book author. I was a teacher, and Clyde Robert Bulla came to our school and visited my eager first grade students. I was as excited as the students and felt tremendously honored to have a chance to meet someone whose work I greatly admired. How fortunate, I thought, were my students to meet him at such an early age. Even as an adult, it was really my first time to think in a personal and meaningful way about authors and the process they went through to write a book. I realized that what authors did seemed quite different to me than the writing process I had learned or was taught to share with my students. That first experience, more than twenty years ago, convinced me that author visits were an important, irreplaceable component of a strong literacy program and reflective of a quality writing program.

When children are learning the tools they need for written communication, an author visit provides them with the opportunity to meet and talk with a person who uses those tools professionally, recording words on paper to inform and entertain. A visit by a children's author can be a rewarding and memorable learning opportunity. Children connect with the author as they develop an understanding of the process of writing and its final completed product. An author can fascinate, surprise, entertain, and inform. Children, as well as adults, respond to authors and their stories with delight, sadness, excitement, and other emotions. Each author's presentation is unique. Some presentations reflect a quiet, informative teaching style, and others entertain with dramatic storytelling and performance flair. Each style can provide an important contribution to the literacy program. An author visit promotes reading and illuminates the reading and writing connection. It can prompt pre- and post-visit literacy activities. Children respond to writing that was done by a person they have had the opportunity to meet with personally. They learn the stories behind the stories they have read. They hear how an author got an idea, developed that seed of an idea into a completed manuscript, and how the book was published. They use that information to inform their own writing and inspire their creativity.

Authors' school visits with groups of students have become increasingly popular. The planning and implementation of an author visit is, however, both a science and an art. This book will assist in the planning and implementation of an author visit. It was prompted by friends and people I've never met who contacted me in person or by phone asking how they could arrange an author visit at their school, for their library, or for a professional organization. They knew I had organized many author visits, and they didn't know where to begin in organizing theirs. I often felt that my responses were too quick and too simple. I knew that author visits were critical and essential to student learning and that my response should be full and complete to ensure a successful visit. I wanted their experience with an author visit to be as satisfying and rewarding as possible.

This book will respond to those inquiries and take the mystery and confusion out of organizing an author visit. As educators, we continually seek the best professional resources to teach us how to assist our students in a variety of ways. An author's visit should be as carefully planned and as researched as any other instructional activity. It is my hope that this resource will assist educators in developing author visits that are meaningful, connected to the learning at the school site, and an important part of the literacy program.

Although I use the term *author* most frequently throughout the book, the information relates to both children's book authors and illustrators. I've simply chosen to use the word *author* more frequently for easier reading. Although I place the setting for most of the author and illustrator visits at a school site, the same process can be used in a public library setting or any other setting that could bring authors and illustrators together with children. In fact, the same strategies can be used to organize an author visit with a group of adults for a professional conference or in other settings where adults and authors meet together. I have chosen to use the terms *author* and *school* to make the content clearer, but authors and illustrators in schools, libraries, and other settings, for all age and grade levels, are an important resource for our children and adults as readers and as writers.

In writing this resource, I wanted it to have "heart." I wanted to move beyond the nuts and bolts of how to coordinate an author visit step-by-step, and to provide readers with anecdotes, stories, and comments that would provide illustrative examples of what I was describing. I'm overwhelmed by the generous contributions of authors and illustrators who gave me valuable insights, stories, doodles, great ideas, and more to share with you. I'm certain that you'll find their responses interesting, informative, heartwarming, silly, surprising, and always enjoyable. I appreciate their support and enthusiasm for this project. They felt it was a needed resource. I hope you agree.

CHAPTER ONE

Let's Start with "Why?"

I've visited a lot of schools that have been super prepared for an author visit. Often, they probably know more about my books and about me than I do myself. These are the schools that are a pleasure to go to because they know the author visit will reinforce the classroom work of teachers and it will multiply the enthusiasm for reading and writing that sometimes seems limited to the school environment. An author visit gives children a chance to see that what they're learning in school applies to the real world. It also gives them a chance to see another adult—somebody from outside the school's walls—who values reading and writing. Finally—and this is very important to me—an author visit gives a school the chance to make literacy as celebrated as football or baseball. Schools that fail to prepare for an author visit really miss an opportunity to make literacy special.

—LARRY DANE BRIMNER

Promoting Literacy

Inviting an author to speak with students speaks volumes about the importance you as teachers, librarians, administrators, and an entire school staff place on literacy, learning, and becoming lifelong readers and writers. You are showing students that writing and reading are important. We learn to read by reading and to read better by reading more. An author visit provides a specific and unique reason for reading, think-

> A fourth or fifth grader recently asked me about beginning a sentence with *and* or *but.* I explained that his teacher was correct, that the official rules say you're not supposed to begin sentences with these words. It was clear, however, that this child knew that the rule is routinely broken. So I added: "Once you understand the rules, then you're allowed to break them."
>
> He thought about that for a few beats, then he said, "There's a name for that."
>
> "Yes," I said. "It's called poetic license."
>
> He shook his head. "Man," he said, "you need a license for everything nowadays."
>
> —LARRY DANE BRIMNER, author of numerous fiction and nonfiction books including *If Dogs Had Wings; Cat on Wheels;* and *Merry Christmas, Old Armadillo.* (www.brimner.com)

ing about the reading, and questioning the writing. Authors make a clear connection between the writer, the writing process, and the final written product. Preparing to meet an author by reading the author's books provides a reading opportunity with a very specific and meaningful purpose. Authors assist teachers, librarians, staff members, family members, and students in increasing their knowledge of children's literature. What better way to truly savor a book than to learn about its creation from the author's point of view? What better way to celebrate literacy than to meet and talk with the people who create the books we read?

The planning for an author visit should start with a clear understanding or purpose for the visit. Author visits provide support for writing programs. Students hear that there is a process to writing that involves persistence as well as creativity. Some authors show their "sloppy copies" and share how they move from those first rough drafts, through multiple revisions, until they have a finished manuscript and ultimately a published book. An author creates meaning with words on a daily basis and uses the rules of grammar. Students will value an opportunity to learn how some people use their writing in their careers. Grammar and spelling are tools of the trade for the author. Plot, character development, point of view, literary devices, and so on are concerns of a writer, not simply a discussion or lesson during a language arts, grammar, or English period at school. Having authors and illustrators visit offers role models to our students as future writers and creators of art.

Real, Live Authors

It's amazing how often I've heard the words *real* or *real, live* when describing an author visit. We typically don't hear the words *a real, live secretary*, or a *real, live lawyer*, or a *real, live doctor*. I'm not certain I know why this happens. Perhaps it is because of the magical quality of books and because people may not come into contact with authors on a regular basis. Maybe it's because, as adults, we are meeting our first "real" and "live" author, and we've typically thought of authors as historical figures when we've studied them in our former English classes. Perhaps it is because we hold them in celebrity status, although we don't say *real, live actor* or *real, live football player*. For whatever reason, adults and children alike are eager to meet a "real, live" author. Here is how Johanna Hurwitz came to the realization that authors were "real" people:

> I grew up believing that all authors were dead. That meant that they had been very old and written their books in the past. I secretly wished that I could be an author even if I didn't meet those criteria. Then one day a friend recommended *Heidi* to me. I checked the book out of the library and loved it, just as my friend had told me I would. But just as exciting as the story, I discovered my name, or at least part of it, on the title page: Johanna Spyri. I covered the author's second name with my hand and stared and stared at the wonder of my name on a book. Just maybe, even if I wasn't dead, I could become an author after all.
>
> —JOHANNA HURWITZ (from *Books Change Lives*, Chicago, IL: ALA Publication, 1994)

Long-Lasting Impressions

Long after the author has visited, students remember the author and the books. They read and reread the author's books and maintain an interest and attachment to the author's work. Many years ago, I had the opportunity to take author and illustrator Kathryn Hewitt to visit a small school in San Diego. *The Three Sillies* had been recently published, and

Author visits are valuable because children see that authors are real people, people who were kids once (many authors like to talk about their childhoods), who have families, homes and pets, who make mistakes (I always talk about my mess-ups), and people who have to take advice and suggestions from their editors and art directors (just like kids get feedback from their teachers).

I always stress that books are really handmade creations, which go through many stages and revisions—and don't just come out finished and perfect-looking on the first try. I hope this gives kids the feeling that, if they love storytelling and art, they can become authors and illustrators, too.

Author visits are also valuable because it's intriguing and fun to see the person who created a book you love. (I know I love to hear and see my favorite authors and illustrators.)

—ELISA KLEVEN, author and illustrator of *The Paper Princess, The Puddle Pail, The Lion and the Little Red Bird, A Monster in the House,* and *Sun Bread* and illustrator of *Abuela, De Colores,* and *City of Angels.* (www.elisakleven.com)

she entertained and informed, sharing pig items that she had collected in response to the pig characters in the book. She even wore a pig nose to look like some of the characters in her book. Many years later, I ran into one of those students we had visited; she was now attending graduate school to become a librarian. She commented to me that she remembered when "The Pig Lady" had visited the school. The student still had a strong memory of that special day when Kathryn Hewitt had visited the school and talked about writing and illustrating. Here's some insight into school visits from Kathryn Hewitt:

One of the reasons I chose to become a writer/illustrator was because of the luxury of spending long hours alone getting paid to daydream. Imagine my horror when I discovered part of the job of being an "author" entailed public speaking to assemblies of

Drawing by Kathryn Hewitt, from *A Taste of Literacy*.

school children. Being a shy person by nature this terrified me more than being Bambi in a forest filled with overzealous NRA members. Speak? In front of hundreds of children? Well, after a couple of years of begging people to let me speak for free, that way if I passed out I was spared the embarrassment of returning their honorarium, I found I actually enjoyed it. I discovered they love it when you tell them you make mistakes, too—so many that I use an electric eraser. They also cheer when you draw pictures for them. And they really guffaw when you show slides of yourself in ridiculous and compromising situations.

Over the years I've shown slides in all sorts of places. One of my favorite places was the interior walls of a castle (to high school students in Oberweisel, Germany). I've also shown my slides in an elementary school hallway, on a wall with exposed pipes above the entry to the boys' bathroom. The intermittent flushing sounds throughout my talk made for great comic relief. I've visited hundreds of schools in the past sixteen years and I'm still humbled by the generosity of the teachers and librarians who took the time and trouble to bring me to their school. Now when I'm working alone for hours in my studio thinking up ideas or getting them down on paper, I see the faces of kids I've met at assemblies sitting on the hard floor, laughing at my dumb jokes. It's the best way to recharge your batteries.

—KATHRYN HEWITT, illustrator of Godiva and the Lives of series, including Lives of the Musicians: Good Times, Bad Times (and What the Neighbors Thought); Lives of the Artists; Lives of the Presidents; and Lives of Extraordinary Women.

Establish a Tradition of Author Visits

Many schools have not yet established a tradition of author visits. Now is the time to make that dedication of time and financial commitment to author visits and the valuable contributions they can make to your school. Bring a "real, live author" to your school each year to motivate reading and writing and to support your literacy program. As you enjoy reading the stories throughout this resource about authors visiting schools, I hope that they will illustrate the importance of an author visit and that you'll soon have an abundance of author visit stories about the impact they have made on individual students and teachers as well as the entire school population.

CHAPTER TWO

What Does an Author Visit Look Like?

The best school visits make me feel like family. The kids have
heard my poems and picture books many times, shared by you.
Like cousins who have never met each other, we are ready!

—JANET S. WONG

There are probably as many variations of an author visit as there
are authors. Authors are storytellers on paper, and some authors
are great storytellers in person as well. Other authors do not share
their information with great dramatic flair or with high performance technique. No matter what their style, authors share what
they do each day and tell how they got an idea and moved it from
the idea to their final manuscript. Perhaps they'll show students
the multitude of drafts they wrote to develop one short picture
book story, or talk about the rejection they have encountered along
the way; talk about their journey toward their career in writing,
and tell of their future aspirations or work. They'll probably talk
about the creative as well as the technical aspects of writing. Their
presentation may combine a variety of segments and include a
show-and-tell time during which they share items related to their
writing or book publication, followed by a slide presentation, perhaps some audience interaction, and time for questions or a reading of their work.

"Where do you get your imagination?"

—Third-grade student to ELISA KLEVEN, illustrator of *The Paper Princess*. (www.elisakleven.com)

The Author Visit Day

An author visit can consist of an author making a visit to individual classrooms, large group assemblies, or workshops where the writer works directly with small or large groups of students. The day may include book sales and an autograph session. You and your author, communicating together, decide how to configure the day. Although you may have come up with your ideal plan for the day, listen to the author and get input from him or her. Roland Smith (www.rolandsmith.com) explains it this way, "The school may plan one or two author visits a year. The author they're inviting may go to one hundred schools a year. Authors know which presentations work best with different age groups. Ask for the author's suggestions and follow their advice. There's a reasonably good chance they know exactly what they're doing."

When I was in elementary school we didn't have author visits. (In fact, we didn't have a library). I loved books and wanted to be an author when I grew up. Because I had never met an author, I thought they were heroic figures of genius with supernatural powers. If I'd had an author visit my school it would have had a profound effect on me. I would have realized that authors are actually just human beings like me and therefore I could become one too. An author visit opens up a world of possibilities. "If I can write a book you can write a book" is one of my messages. "If you can read you can do anything" is another.

—ROLAND SMITH, a nature and novel writer whose works include *Jaguar*, *Sasquatch*, and *Zach's Lie*. (www.rolandsmith.com)

Multiple Author Visits

You may be interested in organizing multiple author visits, bringing an author to each of the schools in your district during a single month. Perhaps you will be interested in bringing numerous authors and students to one central location. The Greater San Diego Reading Association and the San Diego County Office of Education, for example, have worked collaboratively for almost thirty years, bringing thousands of students each year from public and private schools throughout the San Diego area to visit with authors. Each year, a flyer is distributed listing the available authors for each of two days of the Authors' Fair, listing the authors' titles and appropriate grade levels. Teachers review the flyer and register their classes to visit with an author. To accommodate students who are unable to attend because of geographic location or limited funding for buses, one author session is presented via teleconference and broadcast throughout the area on the instructional television channel.

If you are a media specialist, coordinator of library media services, or other person working in a central office position and interested in author visits and literacy, it may be more efficient to provide author visits to numerous schools during a specific period (e.g., March) or to provide author visits throughout the year to various schools throughout an area. Once you've hosted numerous visits, you'll be a valuable asset to others who are looking to arrange visits, and organizing author visits through a central office is more efficient.

The most unusual question I've been asked is from a junior high student who said, "Why don't you write a book about kids being sexually abused by an older kid?" Which just goes to show that there are some very serious things on kids' minds that they want help with—from books.

—JEAN FERRIS, a young adult author of *Across the Grain, Bad, Eight Seconds, Looking for Home,* and *Love Among the Walnuts.* (jferris1@aol.com)

Other Options

Some bookstore owners bring authors to their stores. This practice is frequently organized by publishers to promote an author's book, and some stores encourage student visits with the author. Check to see if your local bookstore provides this type of programming. If not, it's still possible that something can be arranged for your class. Just ask, and see if they've considered this service. This is an especially valuable idea if you have never had the chance to hear an author visit with students, as it will provide you with more insight into this concept. Visiting a bookstore reduces the expense of an author visit, as the only item to budget for is transportation to and from the school and bookstore, which might be a much shorter distance from the author's home to the school.

While planning the author visit, you may wish to consider the contribution an author can make to your staff or parents and consider scheduling a workshop or presentation for adults after school or in the evening. A writing workshop can serve as an outstanding inservice for adults. Some authors encourage parents to bring their children to the family programs or literacy evenings.

Authors in April

Authors in April is a collaborative project of the Rochester Hills Public Library, participating Rochester Community Schools, the Rochester PTA council, and several parochial schools. Four authors visit the Rochester area for one week each April. The authors represent kindergarten to grade one, grades two and three, grades four and five, and grades six to eight. The authors speak to children in the schools, attend an autograph signing session at the library, and

---

My most memorable question came from a middle school student in Texas. After hearing me talk about discriminatory laws against the Chinese, I was asked why I could be so patriotic in view of the unfair treatment. I still don't have an answer to that one.

—MILLY LEE (nimlee.aol.com)

speak at a dinner for adults called Dine with Authors in April. The project is funded by a variety of sources including the public library, the schools' PTA, and local businesses. For more information about this author project, including a listing of each of the authors who have visited in previous years, consult their website at www.rhpl.org/AuthorsinApril.html. There are links to many of the authors' and illustrators' websites.

Schedule the Day

Your author will have input into how the day should be organized, but authors usually prefer not to make more than four presentations in one day, sometimes fewer, with presentations ranging from 30 minutes for younger students to an hour for older students (including time for their questions). If time has been left for questions, it becomes especially important that the questions are meaningful and are prepared in advance. You'll also need to schedule time for autographing of books. Perhaps you will want the author or illustrator to meet with a small group of students who have a focus on writing or illustrating. Some authors offer writing workshops or demonstrations. This typically means that the audience size needs to be reduced.

Plan time for lunch and time for breaks between presentations for the author—time that is not filled with questions or autographing, but for the author to reorganize materials, take a sip of water, run to the bathroom, or catch a breath. Fifteen minutes for a break is usually adequate. Do not add more responsibilities or additional presentations to the author's day. Authors are kind individuals, and it's hard to say "no" to making a "quick stop by the kindergarten class" without looking difficult or unaccommodating. Once you have decided on the schedule with the author, stick to it.

Question: "How much of your books does your dog write?"

Answer: "He's pretty busy, but usually about one-third. Less in the summer when the weather's good."

—ROLAND SMITH, from an actual student interaction (www.rolandsmith.com)

An Author Visit Day

This is only a sampling. Everything in Daniel Pinkwater's *Author's Day* has happened to me.

Getting to the school:

So I'm driving down the road to the Lincolnville (Maine) Elementary School using the map and directions they sent. As I approach the center of the village my directions say, "Turn left at Petunia Pump." I'm thinking what in the world is a Petunia Pump, and looking around. I see a gazebo and slow down to see if there's a pump anywhere in the vicinity. I look up at the lettering on a large handmade cardboard sign on the gazebo's post and read, "Yes Bruce, this is Petunia Pump."

Arriving at the school:

I pull into the elementary school in Chagrin Falls, Ohio. I know I'm at the right school when I see the sign, "Welcome Bruce McMillan" and I'm a minute early. I unload and wheel my speaking pack to the office. It's quiet. The only person around is the school secretary at her desk. "Good morning, I believe I'm expected. I'm Bruce McMillan." She just looks at me and doesn't say anything. It becomes a bit awkward. I finally say, "Perhaps you could direct me to where the presentation will be." She replied in a monotone, "The gym's over there," and pointed across the hall. So I go over to the gym and set up.

What I didn't know was that one of the teachers' husbands had come by five minutes earlier to leave something off for his wife. Upon his arrival, the official greeting committee of the principal, PTA president, and host teacher had all looked at him, then at each other, and said to him, "Are you Bruce McMillan?" Without missing a beat, he looked back at them and said, "Yes." Then they all proceeded on a tour of the school. Finally, while I'm setting up a very amused and embarrassed group of three races in to greet me. I'm not sure I would've wanted to be that teacher's husband when he got home that day.

During the presentation:

At the elementary school in Atkinson, New Hampshire grades kindergarten, one and two arrive for my first morning assembly. The gym is full. One of my opening comments is, "I know that you won't talk while I'm talking." And I pause while the kids all nod their heads. "But would you let me know if the teachers talk while I'm talking?" The kids all smile. You can hear them thinking, "I like this idea."

So we're having a great time and when I ask them a question the kids are raising their hands to win a bookmark or postcard. I'm all over the room with my lapel wireless mike. Nobody is too far away. Halfway through the presentation a boy in the front is waving his arm even though I haven't asked a question. I try to ignore it, but this young man is not to be denied. Finally I go over to him and quietly say, "What is it?" He replies not so quietly, "Mrs. (name deleted) is talking," and he turns to look at her. I also look over there, as does everyone else in the gym. The room gets very quiet, as we all watch Mrs. (name deleted) chatting with another teacher. They were chatting away. We are all watching and finally the two teachers look out to see why it's so quiet all of a sudden in the gym. Only then do they realize everyone is looking at them. I say, "And I have a bookmark for you for following my instructions," and I give it to the student. The two teachers didn't have a clue as to why that student won a bookmark, though I think they may have found out later.

After the presentation:
My favorite question came from a third grader in Ohio.
"Have you ever been in jail?"
"I'll tell you the truth," and I paused. The teachers' eyes popped. The kids were all ears. "The answer is yes." The teachers' jaws dropped. "And it happened many many years ago, at least the first time." I paused. It was so quiet. Did I ever have everyone's attention.
"Here's what happened." I paused again and then finished the thought. "I landed on this spot and I had to go to jail. I had to go directly to jail. I couldn't go past "GO" and I couldn't collect $200." The teachers' eyes rolled. The kids mumbled. "Oh I get it, Monopoly."
As authors we get so many predictable questions that when we get a new one it almost startles us. My thrill in this one was that I came up with my answer without missing a beat.

After the visit:
I received this student's letter. "My great great uncle Robert Frost was a writer. He would have wanted probably to meet you. P.S. You're the best! Sarah." This was in New Hampshire and the teacher added a comment that Sarah truly was a descendant of the noted New Hampshire poet Robert Frost.

—BRUCE MCMILLAN is the author of numerous books, including *Growing Colors*, *The Weather Sky*, and *Mouse Views: What the Class Pet Saw*. (www.brucemcmillan.com)

Are There Any Questions?

Many authors provide some time at the end of the program to allow students the opportunity to ask questions. This personal time provides students with the chance to ask questions that are important to them. Their questions vary and might be personal, about the author's family, about writing, or about being a writer. Students are frequently curious to know how much an author gets paid or how old an author is. Authors, especially for older students, may explain the royalty system. The more prepared students are, the more insightful their questions and the more linked they will be to the real business at hand—concerns about reading and writing.

> I will always remember my first author visit. A fifth grader raised his hand and asked, "What are your long-term aspirations for your career?" I blundered through that one, still working then on the question of whether or not I was a writer.
>
> I have great respect for kids. One fourth grader told me he liked to write. "Oh, that's great. What kind of writing do you do?" "Oh," he said, "I prefer writing comedy." Author Visit Rule #1— Never underestimate the intelligence of kids.
>
> —MARY CASANOVA, author of picture books through young adult novels including *The Hunter, One Dog Canoe, Moose Tracks, Wolf Shadows, Riot,* and *Stealing Thunder.*
> (www.marycasanova.com)

Here's one technique for a nervous author to accommodate questions:

> At one school I go to, I get to ask the kids questions. ("Did you always want to be a fifth grader?" "Where do fifth graders get their ideas?") The strategy is obvious: I get them to answer their own questions—and then we discuss how being a writer is/isn't like being a fifth grader.
>
> —KATE KLISE (KateKlise@aol.com)

A few years ago, I was speaking about reptiles to a group of K–2s and a little girl raised her hand and asked, "How do snakes make babies?" I looked at the teachers for some guidance, but none of them wanted anything to do with the question, so I launched right in. What was so interesting was that the kids were absolutely fine with the explanation. A couple of them giggled, but most just nodded their heads, accepting it as just one more interesting aspect of life.

Afterward, several teachers came up to me and said, "We are so glad YOU got that question and not us!" The point, perhaps, is that if you just shoot straight with kids, you can often teach them things during an author visit that regular instructors could not get away with. A footnote to this story is that little girl's question gave me an inspiration for my book *Making Animal Babies*. It's not the first time I've heard of authors getting book ideas during school visits.

—SNEED B. COLLARD III, author of numerous nonfiction books in the science area, including *Animal Dads*, *Leaving Home*, *The Forest in the Clouds*, and *Butterfly Count*. (www.author-illustr-source.com/sneedcollard.htm)

How Old Are You?

Some authors are asked the question "how old are you?" perhaps because it's the first question we typically ask a child, or maybe as a way to get a little more personal with the author.

A Countdown of Wacky Anonymous Questions

10. How do you make the covers for the book?
9. Where do you buy your underwear?
8. Could you come home with me after school to play?
7. Now that you have written all these books, don't you think it is time you became a principal?
6. (After explaining the royalty system to a group of fifth graders) "Why would you want to be an author when there's so many better paying jobs in America?"
5. When are you going to write a real book?
4. How can I get boys to like me? (from a second-grade girl)
3. Will you be my mother?
2. Can I star in your next book?
1. Have you ever won the Blueberry Award?

Uh, author lady? Are you afraid you'll get too old and won't be able to have children?

—Contributed by KATE KLISE, author of novels that are illustrated
by her sister, M. Sarah Klise, including *Letters from Camp*,
Regarding the Fountain: A Tale in Letters, *Of Liars and Leaks*, and
Trial by Journal.

"Are you young?" To which, of course, I replied, "Yes." (I'm 42.)

—KATIE DAVIS (www.katiedavis.com)

"Is that your natural hair color?" My response, once I'd recovered: "It used to be."

—CYNTHIA DEFELICE, writer and storyteller for a variety of age
levels; her work includes *Casey in the Bath*, *Weasel*, and
Death at Devil's Bridge. (www.cynthiadefelice.com)

Mary Downing Hahn answered the question of age and was met by a concerned girl of ten who told her, "My mother says a true lady never reveals her age." (Mary is a writer of outstanding novels, including *Anna All Year Round*, *December Stillness*, *Time for Andrew: A Ghost Story*, and *Wait till Helen Comes*. (www.carr.org/authco/hahn.htm)

Ask the Author!

It's Author Day at school. We've looked at edited manuscripts, proofs and illustrations. We've talked about ideas and rewriting. We've seen incidents from real life appear in books. The time has come—that unpredictable fifteen minutes between "any questions?" and "I think we're about out of time." Hundreds of kids sit on the floor of the media center waving hands wildly. In front of the crowd an author stands, hoping that no one will ask the dreaded question, "How old are you?" Teachers wait in the back of the room wringing their hands.

"Any questions?"

With kindergarten students, the questions are statements. My dog had puppies. I lost my lunch ticket. They are so eager to share their own stories that they forget themselves in their enthusiasm. But the first grader knows enough about what a question is to say, "Did you know my dog had puppies?" "Did you know I lost my lunch ticket?" They are very concerned with the actual construction of the book. How do you get the cardboard on? How do you paint on the front?

Often at the beginning of the session the questions show a distorted view of the author. Do you ride in a limo? Do you know Tom Cruise? Are you famous? When writer and child interact something wonderful happens. Children begin to see the writer as a real person. The questions move away from the questions about the author's "celebrity" status to the writing. Where do you get your ideas? How to you make the characters real?

Questions reflect curiosity about the creative process at all levels. A first grader confesses: I can do the stories, I just can't do the words. I sympathize. I have that trouble, too. I tell him writing is nothing more than telling stories except that we put them down on paper and writing words down is the hardest part. A fourth grader asks, "What if you can't get an idea?" If I'm blocked I get my creative juices flowing other ways. I read good books, or sew, or bake and soon I'm running to my computer with a new idea. Is your job boring? Never. How could I get bored riding roller coasters, fighting bullies, and waging war with a food fight catapult?

How do you know when a book is done? I quote my mother, "It's finished when it sounds like you haven't worked on it at all." The questions go on and on.

In older grades, students ask me some questions about symbolism or foreshadowing but most of the questions are personal. They are striving to see the writer as a person. They want to know about our pets and if our children play baseball, what our favorite foods are and what we do in our spare time. They ask about our childhoods and favorite books. Most of all they want to know what makes an author sit down at a computer every morning to write stories and they want to know if they can do it, too. In the questions they are seeking affirmation that they can be writers, that their own struggles with words are valid.

Somewhere in that fifteen minutes is the true exchange of reader and writer, the rare chance for the reader of a book to confront the writer of the book and ask them anything. It's also a chance for a writer to hear first hand their audience's reaction to the books.

I'm always a little sorry to say, "I think we're just about out of time."

—BETSY DUFFEY is the author of *Fur-Ever Yours*, *Booker Jones* and *My Dog, My Hero* (a joint project with her mother and sister).
(www.betsyduffey.com)

Dear Author, Where Do You Get Your Ideas?

Adults and children alike enjoy learning the story behind the story. "Where do you get your ideas?" is the question I've heard most frequently asked to authors during author visits and in one-on-one conversations.

People of all ages are interested in knowing how an idea for a book is developed. The stories behind the stories are as different and as interesting as the authors and their books. The question is really one about the creative process and is not a simple one to answer. When students (not to mention adults) hear how a seed of an idea takes shape, they feel like insiders, privy to what authors do and how they create. They may see potential for their own writing. I wanted to include a story behind a story for this resource. Why? Because I think it's important to give an illustrative example of what I mean by learning the story behind the story. The story behind *Frindle* is a perfect fit because it shows how an idea was started; because it took place during an author visit; and because it's a great literacy story and author visits are all about literacy and promoting the love of reading, writing, and words. Andrew Clements describes how he got the idea for his popular *Frindle* on a school visit, but don't expect that an author will get an idea from your school visit or will feature you and your school in his or her next book.

The Story behind the Story *Frindle* by Andrew Clements

I found the idea for *Frindle* almost by accident. I was talking to a bunch of second grade kids one October afternoon in 1990 at the JFK Elementary School in Middletown, Rhode Island. I was teaching a little about the way words work, and about what words really are. I was trying to explain to them how words only mean what we decide they mean. They didn't believe me when I pointed to a fat dictionary and told them that ordinary people like them and like me had made up all the words in that book and that new words get made up all the time.

I pulled a pen from my pocket and said, "For example, if all of us right here today said we would never call this thing a 'pen' again, and that from now on we would call it a . . . frindle, then in five or ten years, frindle could be a real word in the dictionary." I just made up the word frindle, and they all laughed because it sounded funny.

There was one boy in the back of the room who didn't believe me. He frowned and shook his head, and said, "Nah, that's impossible. You can't just make up a new word and have other people start using it."

So I said, "OK. There's a store down the street from the school where you go buy candy, right? So walk in there after school today, put 79 cents on the counter, look right at the person behind the counter and say, 'I need to buy a frindle.' That person is going to look at you like you're crazy, but say the word again 'a frindle.' Say it two or three more times, and then point at the plastic container of pens. Next day, have a different kid go in the store and ask the same person for a frindle. Skip a day, and have a different friend do the same thing. Six days later when the fifth kid comes and asks for a frindle, what's that person behind the counter going to do?"

Well, that kid in the back of the room was right with me, and he got the idea. I could see it in his face. He raised his hand and he blurted out, "He's going to ask if you want a blue one or a black one!" That boy understood that for that person in the store, frindle would be a real word. It would mean pen.

The kids loved that story, and for a couple of years I told that same story every time I went to talk at a school or a library. Then one day as I was sifting through my life, looking for a story idea, I wondered what would happen if a kid really did start using a new word, and other kids really liked it, but his English teacher didn't. So the idea for the book was born, and I even used that bit about the store as part of the novel.

Before I Come to Visit

Think of me as family
make me the grump
      the hungry sister
      the busy buzzzzy mother
      the cousin who dreams

I don't want to be the kind of boring company
you have to sweep the floor for
sit perfectly still and listen to
on and on and on and on until
f i n a l l y I'm gone—

When we meet
I want you to run up and shout hello
since you have known me already
for months

Then we can just jump on in
and catch up on family stories
big crazy hopes
secrets

I keep my suitcase packed
at all times—

Are you ready?

> —JANET WONG is a poet and author of books and poetry collections
> for all grade levels, including *Good Luck Gold, Suitcase of Seaweed,*
> *The Rainbow Hand, BUZZ, This Next New Year, The Trip Back*
> *Home, Behind the Wheel, Night Garden,* and *GRUMP.* (At her
> website, www.janetwong.com, you can listen to Janet tell
> wonderful stories and read her magical poems.)

CHAPTER THREE

Finding and Inviting Your Author

An author's visit is a comet with a long and brilliant tail. Long before I arrive, kids and teachers across the grades are reading my books. A "buzz" is created. The author visit day is highly charged, full of energy and excitement. I show slides and talk about the stories behind my stories, my writing process and writing tips, and remind kids that they have stories only they can write. The real benefit comes after I leave. Kids read more and talk more about books, and as importantly, they're writing their own stories. (Fan letters and thank you's come across my desk when I return, telling me so.)

A comet gets our attention. We watch for it long before it arrives, gather together on the day it passes, and talk about it after it's gone. A good author visit does the same thing, helping to build a long-lasting community of readers and writers.

—Mary Casanova

Designing Your Day

Okay. You're sold. You know that an author visit will be valuable to your reading and writing program. You've seen its purpose and worth to your students and staff. Perhaps you've even known that you would like to bring an author to your school for a long time. Now what? Here are some basic questions to think about as you begin to plan your

I am continually amazed and moved by the imagination and energy of teachers. My goodness—what a hard job that has to be. I try to help them teach in a small way by sharing what I do and leaving each audience with an open-ended story to finish. I've been told many times that classes can't wait to sit down and finish the story. I also hope that if even one child looks at me and what I do and says to herself, "I could do that!" my visit has been valuable. Many children love art and writing but are discouraged from thinking of them as careers. Seeing someone who happily makes her living doing those things can be reassuring and empowering.

—ASHLEY WOLFF, illustrator of the popular *Miss Bindergarten* series, including *Miss Bindergarten Gets Ready for Kindergarten*, *Miss Bindergarten Celebrates the 100th Day of Kindergarten*, *Miss Bindergarten Stays Home from Kindergarten*, and *Miss Bindergarten Takes a Field Trip with Kindergarten*. (www.ashleywolff.com)

day. Don't worry if you don't know all of the answers now, but the questions will help you start to formulate your author day visit.

Who   Who do you want to invite? Who will be the audience? Find an author who is grade- and interest-level appropriate. Who will organize the visit (teacher, principal, media specialist, reading specialist, parent volunteer)? Be sure the person organizing the visit can get the support of all the staff to ensure a successful visit.

What   What do you want the author to do? Many authors have a variety of programs and presentations to provide based on the age of the audience and on their interest. The more information you can provide to the author, the better "fit" will be the presentation. Sessions with kids? Teachers? Community members? Other libraries? Bookstores? What is the purpose of the visit?

When Specific date, or general time (e.g., February, or spring)

Where Confirm your location now. (A quiet place if using A/V equipment; also, will the room darken enough to success-fully show slides or video?)

Why Have a clear purpose. What do you want to achieve? This will help you in identifying funding and will be helpful to you as you develop publicity to make it clear to your community why you are having an author visit.

How How long will the presentation be, and how many presen-tations will there be? How large will the groups be?

Money, Money, Money

Budget constraints always seem to be a black cloud hovering over the educational program. Money always seems to be a problem. An au-thor visit isn't icing on the cake, an enjoyable break from the in-structional day, or a frill. It's not enrichment. It's an important, inte-gral part of the instructional program and its literacy activities and should be approached just that way. Money can be "found" if you desire it. If this is your first time to invite an author, you may have a more difficult time finding financial support; however, after the first successful and well-planned author visit, it will become clear to all staff members and parents how important an author visit is to the lit-eracy program. In future years, generating funding will become eas-ier based on the success of the first visit, and funding can be ear-marked on a yearly basis for this express purpose. Determine possible funding sources. Schools have funds that can be budgeted for school visits. Many educators apply for grants to obtain funds. Book fairs and PTA fund-raising activities can be allocated.

Costs

There are a number of factors that will impact your total visit cost. Authors and illustrators have their own fees, and their honorarium varies. Total cost depends on a variety of conditions and on the de-tails of the visit, and the amount of travel will also impact the total cost of the visit. You are responsible for arranging and paying for the author's travel and local accommodation expenses. How many presentations, how far the author lives from the school site, and how much money will be needed for travel, lodging, and additional expenses will all impact the total cost of the program. And, yes, you need to feed authors, so budget for that as well. A widely known author will cost more than a local author with only one book, making a local author a good choice for budgetary reasons. On the other hand, sometimes a well-known author who lives in your area will charge less than he or she would to go out of state, because speaking with students nearby helps an author reduce the amount of total travel time and allows for less time away from home.

If you are bringing an author from a distance, you may be able to collaborate with a local library, other school, local bookstore, professional organization's conference, and so on to share costs. This will help reduce the travel expense cost for each organization. Sometimes authors are on tour to promote their newest book and will be in your area. If there is a local, regional, or state conference coming to your area, contact them and see if you can coordinate with one of their author presenters for an author visit. As the author will already be in the area, this will reduce the total cost of the school visit by reducing travel and housing expenses.

Here are some more budget ideas:

- Look at categorical funding sources, and determine how special funding can support an author's visit.
- Develop the support of your parent association for the program. Parent organizations are often willing to help with the logistics and the funding of an author visit.
- Develop a partnership in the community. Some community groups are very willing to support special programs when asked.
- Ask local service clubs (e.g., Kiwanis or Rotary). Service organizations are often interested in sponsoring special and highly visible projects.
- Develop a partnership with a local business or businesses.
- Use profits from book fairs, if they are not currently being used to sponsor book purchases or other literacy activities.
- Team up with another school, educational organization, or local bookstore to share travel expenses to reduce each school's total cost.

- Collaborate with a local council of the International Reading Association, National Council of Teachers of English, library organization, or other literacy group to bring an author to the area.
- Ask your Friends of the Library group.
- Principals often have money designated for assemblies. What better assembly could there be? Talk with your principal about earmarking a portion of that budget to support an annual author visit.
- Use more than one source of funding if necessary.
- Combine an author visit with staff development for teachers or parents, and use a portion of in-service or staff development money to cover the presentation and expenses.
- Establish that this is an integral part of the instructional program and that there will be a budgetary commitment on an annual basis.

Author Juice Machine

I was at a school that had an "Author's Visit Juice Machine." It was a vending machine maintained by a vending machine company. All the students, teachers, and parents knew that the profits from the machine went towards their annual Author Visit. They averaged $2,500 a year from the one machine. The machine was serviced by the vending company. All the librarian had to do was to go to the bank with the money.

—Roland Smith (www.rolandsmith.com)

How to Find an Author

Start by deciding what type of an author you would like to have visit. Do you want to have an author of picture books, or a writer of novels who will speak to the upper grades only? Do you want a fiction writer or a nonfiction writer? Do you want an illustrator, someone who writes and illustrates, or a writer? How about a poet? Brainstorm with staff members to determine what your needs are and who might be an outstanding choice for a visit. Remember, not all authors and illustrators enjoy making school visits, nor do all authors have the same amount of time budgeted for school visits. Because of professional or personal responsibilities, some authors can't commit to

My visits to schools, especially those with a large number of students from nonwhite communities, present the idea that here is a person of color who is a published author—maybe, it could be something I could do too. I like to think that I present an option of what their lives could be if they want to try it too. My childhood dreams were so limited because I didn't know what else I could be when I grew up. Getting married and living happily ever after was the only option open to me at that time.

In my books, I wanted to present a different perspective—that of an Asian American child who lived during a specific time in history in this country. It was Nim and that paper drive, just like there were paper drives all over the country during World War II. In *Earthquake*, I advance the idea that there was a Chinese community living in San Francisco at that time, and they suffered the same fears too. But, they were not counted officially, so it would seem that no Chinese died or were hurt in the disaster. There were over 6000 Chinese in Chinatown. What happened to them?

—MILLY LEE, author of two outstanding historical fiction picture books, *Nim and the War Effort* and *Earthquake*—both set in San Francisco. (nimlee@aol.com)

as many author visits as other authors. Some authors continue to work full-time or part-time at other jobs, reducing their available time for visits.

The Internet has made it much easier to identify authors who are willing to visit schools. Consult the Internet to see if some of your favorite authors have a website. Many authors have personal websites providing a wealth of information, including details about author visits. Other authors have websites through their publishers, which can provide you with the needed information including the types of programs the author has created or is interested in presenting, contact information, and an overview of his or her published books. Some authors even provide fee information on their websites and often have a listing of frequently asked questions (FAQ), which may be helpful to you as you determine whom to invite and as you do your planning. There are numerous websites that can be helpful in identifying authors. Refer to Website Resources at the back of this book to find outstanding websites that will assist you in finding an author, or type in some of your favorite authors' names on a search engine and see if they have websites and if they are interested in presenting at schools.

To reduce the total cost of having an author visit your school site, you might decide to find someone who lives close or in a nearby state to visit. This is especially true if this is the first author to visit your school. This will reduce the total cost of the author visit by eliminating or reducing the travel expenses. Find out if you have an author who lives in your community and whose work will be an appropriate match for your students.

Do you have a local chapter of the Society of Children's Book Writers and Illustrators? SCBWI is a professional organization for writers and illustrators of children's literature. Their website (www .SCBWI.org) identifies local and regional chapters and contact information. It also has an alphabetical listing of all of its members with links to their websites. Although the SCBWI website is not set up for the purpose of arranging author visits, this is a very useful website. Many regions have a speaker's bureau associated with titles or types of writing or illustrating. Others have direct links to the authors' websites. This includes writers who are just starting their careers but who have been published in children's magazines, have poems and stories to their credit, and have an eagerness and willingness to talk about writing with children. They may not be writers of books you are familiar with now, but they have much to offer your students. They may not have the same level of expertise or amount of experience in working with students as a more accomplished author may have, so they may be interested in talking with only smaller groups of students. This can be an immensely enjoyable experience for students, and a new writer may welcome the chance to talk with his or her potential audience.

Newspaper reporters and columnists are another source of talented local writers. As they are paid a salary by the newspaper, they may be willing to visit a school site for free or for a nominal cost. Many are interested in visiting schools and have much to share with students as they talk about writing, working on their stories, and their writing career. My experiences have been that newspaper columnists have made a wonderful addition to the author visit program. Former San Diegan Brad Anderson, the creator of the *Marmaduke* cartoon, was a welcome addition to my school's program of author visits; perhaps you are lucky and have a local cartoonist in your area. Students are able to see the columnist's work in the newspaper on a regular basis, and teachers can cut and share the columns that they feel students will have the most interest in reading.

Colleagues and Connections

Although the Internet may provide information about whether an author likes to visit schools and the programs authors are able to provide, it's preferable to have had a chance to hear an author before or to have a recommendation by a colleague who has heard the author. A great way to "find" an author is to contact colleagues at other schools to see if they have had an author visit their school in the past. And, if you have never had the opportunity to observe an author presenting to students, try to attend at least one of his or her presentations at another school or to visit the school for the part of the day when the author will be there. This will give you much-needed insight into organizing your big day.

> At a school in Torrance, California, after I had presented some assemblies, a teacher walked up with a child and said, "He would like to give you a hug, if you don't mind." I happily received and returned my hug, and then she went on to explain. The child was not only developmentally challenged but also had come to the school speaking a language other than English and was having a difficult time. She said, "After your assembly, when we went back to the classroom, he picked up your book and started reading, singing the words—he was so excited! He wanted to thank you."
>
> —JOAN BRANSFIELD GRAHAM, a poet and an author of two books on concrete poetry: *Splish Splash* and *Flicker Flash*. (www.joangraham.com)

Ask some of your colleagues (local public librarians, other school librarians, reading specialists, etc.) if they've heard authors or know of authors who would be excellent presenters for your school site. Ask the staff of your local bookstore if there is an author visiting in the future, and see if you can work together with them on an existing tour—or perhaps you can work together to identify an author who can visit both the store and the school. Local bookstores, especially children's bookstores, can be very helpful in identifying authors who live locally or within a fair proximity.

Another way to find an author is to hear one speak at a literacy, library, or other educational conference and find out how he or she can be contacted. After you have heard him or her, you will know a little about the author's presentation style for adults, and this will give you great insight into the presentations of those authors to children. You could find a perfect person for your school site this way.

Do not invite an author unless you have personally read his or her books. An author told me once that he was at a dinner in his honor with librarians from five schools he was to visit and discovered that none of them had read any of his books. They had invited him because they had "heard" he was a good presenter. He is, of course, a fabulous presenter, but what a missed opportunity for these adults.

Publishers

Consider contacting a publisher about arranging an author visit. Many publishers have a list of authors and other information about author visits, and they often have marketing staff who are willing to help you identify an author. Or, you may know which author you would like to invite and can contact that author through his or her publisher. Publishers often develop biographical information packets about their authors to distribute at conferences, stating where an author lives, and others provide a geographic listing of authors in their catalogs or online. You might be surprised the next time you are reading a book to learn that the author lives near you! I've been pleased to learn about many local authors by simply reading the dust jackets of books and noting that the author lives nearby. As a result, I've become a careful observer of author information on dust jackets and other publisher materials, as I'm always looking for new, local talent. Later in your planning process for an author visit, publishers can be helpful by sending biographical information or photos for you to use in your publicity.

I was presenting to fourth graders, and they had asked me all kinds of questions about being famous, etc. One kid in the back raised his hand. The teacher next to him whispered something and he whispered back. She frowned and shook her head. I had the impression he was not known to be a stellar student. He put his hand down. I told him he could still ask me if he wanted. He said no. The four boys in the rows in front of him must have heard the whispering because they all shouted out: "We'll ask!" The question was, "What kind of car do you have?"

Now I thought this was a great question. The reason is, this kid was looking at me like I was different. I was the author, Rich and Famous and living an unattainable life. I told him, "You too can grow up to be an author and drive an eight-year-old beat up Ford!"

—KATIE DAVIS, author and illustrator of *I Hate to Go to Bed!*, *Who Hops?*, *Who Hoots?*, and *Scared Stiff*. (www.katiedavis.com)

Writing a Letter

You've decided on who you would like to have visit your school. You've gathered some support and you've got some funding. Now what? Inviting an author to visit a school can be as simple as writing a letter or an e-mail. Many authors, especially those who enjoy speaking at schools, have websites through which you can directly e-mail them with your speaking request. If you don't know the author's address or the author doesn't have a personal or publisher website, you may need to write the letter in care of the publisher. The letter serves as a way of communicating to the author about the school, its students, and its reading and writing program. It outlines why the author's visit is an important one to the staff and students of the school. In other words, why do you want this author at your school site?

Write your letter as early as possible, as it is not unusual for an author's schedule to be booked a year in advance. Think your program through before inviting the author, so you can provide the specifics of what you will want for presentations and what questions you have for the author. Unless you have unlimited funding and can host more than one author, invite only one author at a time. It would be very embarrassing to send out multiple requests and have multiple positive responses for the same time slot.

Consider the following list of items to be included in the invitation to the author. Some of the information you may need to determine with the author, but this provides an overview of the details that need to be considered for your letter.

The following items need to be included in an invitation to an author:

- Reasons the school staff and students are interested in having this particular author
- Expectations for the author's visit
- Amount of honorarium the school will be able to pay (determine your budget before you ask your author, or be prepared to find additional funding if necessary)
- Travel expenses the school will pay or ones that will be shared with the local library, bookstore, publisher, etc.
- Date or dates you would like the author to visit (if the date is flexible, note an approximate time; for example, "March" or "this spring")
- Schedule for the day of the visit, including the beginning and ending times for the day and the presentations
- Grade, age level, and size of audiences
- Location(s) of presentations
- Contact information for possible questions the author may have, including a day and evening number
- Return address and the contact person's name
- Self-addressed stamped envelope (if you are extending the invitation by letter and want a written response)

Don't be too disappointed if the author sends regrets. An author needs to balance speaking engagements with school site visits and presentations at professional organizations and with his or her real business—writing. Keep in mind that speaking takes time away from the author's writing, which is the very thing you admire. If you receive a "no" from one author, just decide on another good match for your audience.

Juliahouse Author Tours

c/o **Jennifer Taylor**
6631 Colbert Street
New Orleans, LA 70124
Phone/Fax: (504) 484-6481
E-mail: julhouse@aol.com

Provides professional and educational school visits and conference presentations for renowned authors of children's books, including Brod Bagert and Gary Dulabaum. Call or e-mail for additional information.

A letter can express your creativity and imagination. The following creative letter inviting Mem Fox to Northern California was written by Dr. Barbara Schubert from St. Mary's College and the Santa Clara County Office of Education. It was paired with a more formal letter that provided Mem with the specific details of dates, time, expectations, and so forth. But, this letter captures the heart of the visit and shows the author that she's going to have a great day.

The Not-So-Formal Invitation That Just Wrote Itself!

(with apologies to Dr. Seuss and Mem Fox)

Dear Mem-I-Am, dear Mem-I-Am,
We do so like you, Mem-I-Am,
We like your style, we like your grace,
We like your hair, we like your face.

We like the way you have with words,
With teachers, students—even nerds!
We'd like for you to have your say
On a bright and crisp February day.

The dates are set, the crowds await;
To hear Mem Fox, they won't be late!
Please say you'll be there, rain or sun
We guarantee two days of fun!

You've started identifying the profile of your day, you've identified an author, and you've invited your author. And, more importantly, your author has said, "yes, yes, yes!" Now the nitty-gritty planning begins.

Recipe for a Successful Author Visit

Ingredients:

> 1 author or illustrator, properly selected
> 1–4 groups of finely prepared students
> a pinch of humor
> 2 heaping handfuls of preparation and organization
> 3 scoops of creativity
> a dash of tenderness
> a dollop of ingenuity

Combine all ingredients and carefully stir. Add spice to taste. Flavor improves with age. Sprinkle generously with care and kindness. Serve and enjoy!

Cook's Note: Memories store well and are long-lasting.

CHAPTER FOUR

The Nitty-Gritty Details

An author visit is a cooperative enterprise between the faculty
and the author.

—Brod Bagert

Step-by-Step

Your author has been selected, invited, and said yes, and a committee pulled together. Now what? Here are some basic details and
some interesting anecdotes to inspire and guide your planning. Select and use the information provided within this resource to suit
your needs. Have fun and create your own special day as you complete the nitty-gritty details and move toward the pleasure of host-
ing an author.

Travel and Lodging

If the author will be traveling, who will make those arrangements?
Will you be making the author's travel plans, or will the author? If
you are making them, does the author have preferences such as win-
dow seat or aisle on a plane, or making connections through a particular city? How will the author be getting from the airport to the hotel or school? Assign someone to pick the author up at the airport,
preferably at the gate. It's helpful to meet the author with a sign

bearing his or her name or to have one of his or her books in hand for easy identification.

If the author is driving to the school, provide careful directions. Include a few landmarks. Drive the route yourself to make sure the place names and highway exit numbers are correct. Inaccurate directions may result in the author being late and being stressed. Trust me. I once told an author the directions for how to get to the school based on the route I took. Unfortunately, I didn't know that there wasn't an exit off the highway going south, as I was always going north. Imagine my embarrassment when the very kind author arrived. Whenever possible, pick the author up and drive the author to the school. This ensures that there will be someone to help the author with carrying the presentation materials as well as finding the school office and the room for the presentations. Reserve a parking place for the author with an inviting sign. This is really essential if parking spots are at a premium at your school, as the author will probably be carrying speaking materials.

What kind of hotel room will your author need? Who will be making the reservation? Be sure that it is a quiet, clean, and safe room with an in-room bathroom. Will the author need a smoking or nonsmoking room? Will the author be traveling alone? How many beds? Does the hotel have an Internet hook-up or a work space? (Many authors work on their writing in the evening, even after a long day visiting with students.) Does the hotel have a restaurant nearby to accommodate the meal needs of the author? (A visitor, especially one without a car, will find it inconvenient to track down the nearest place for a bite to eat.) Bed and breakfasts may seem romantic and interesting, but many do not have the basic features authors will need to make their evenings comfortable, including access to food in the evening, appropriate work space, or private in-room telephones. Make arrangements with the hotel for late arrival in case a plane is delayed unexpectedly.

Arrange for the hotel to bill your school or organization directly rather than asking the author to pay the bill and then be reimbursed. Authors may do fifty to 200 visits per year. Imagine the out-of-pocket expenses they would incur if they were asked to pay for all of these and then be reimbursed for expenses. (From a personal point of view, I think the worst room I ever stayed in was one that was reserved by the organization sponsoring my visit. There was no alarm clock, no phone, no place to eat within the building, no trash can, no blanket on the bed, and no heat adjustment for the room. This became a problem for this California girl when it began snowing!) Be certain your author has an appropriate room. It doesn't have to be fancy, but it does need to have the basics.

Pamper your author. An author is away from home and expending great energy to give top-notch presentations. Little things make a big difference. Respect the author's need for quiet and "down time." Little extras such as a welcome note, flowers, a small gift, or fruit in a hotel room are greatly appreciated.

Two Author Visit Stories

"As part of Kern Reading Association's Young Authors' Week in Bakersfield, California, I was invited to speak at Longfellow Elementary, the school I attended as a girl. My parents still live a few blocks from Longfellow, and one of the teachers told me she would pick me up in the morning. A few minutes before the designated time, the doorbell rang and I answered the door. Two first-grade boys stood on the porch, smiling, and one said, "Are you ready for school?" I looked out into my parents' front yard, and an entire class, their teachers, teachers' aides, and assorted parents with baby strollers stood smiling and waiting for me. The teacher had sent home permission slips for the children and invited their parents also to come to school early so they could "walk the author to school the same route she walked to school when she was a little girl." The students took turns holding my hand and pulling my wheeled suitcase with my speaking materials. We walked to the corner and waited for the crossing guard to cross us, exactly as I did years before.

"Did you used to go this way?" the students asked. Yes.

"Is it the same crossing guard?" they wondered. No.

When we got back to the school, an arch had been made out of balloons and big sign that said, "Welcome Back, Pam Muñoz Ryan." My parents were quite touched, like I was. It was a sentimental day I'll never forget.

Another one of my most memorable school visits was Bonner Elementary in South Carolina. The school librarian told me to wait in front of my hotel for a driver to pick me up in the morning. A limousine pulled up. I looked around to see who the celebrity might be waiting behind me.

The driver said, "I'm here to pick up Pam Muñoz Ryan."

I couldn't have been more surprised. When the limo pulled up at the school, the entire student body crowded in a long line next to the curb, cheering wildly and waving little American flags. (In celebration of *The Flag We Love*.) When I stepped out of the limo, a louder cheer erupted from the students. The principal handed me a bouquet of flowers and suggested I walk the length of the lined-up students and shake their hands. I actually got teary-eyed. I don't know who was more exited that day—me or the students. It was a lovely day, very far removed from my typical life.

This school has an author every year. When I walked into the building, I noticed that the halls were named "Eric Carle Blvd" and "Steven Kellogg Lane." By the time I left that day, they had named a hallway after me, too. This school brings their author to school in a different way each year. One year they brought the author in a cherry picker. Another author arrived in a fire engine. Another in an antique car. It's just one more example of the lengths that teachers and schools will seek to make an author visit a memorable experience and exciting for students.

—Pam Muñoz Ryan, author of *Mice and Beans*, *Amelia and Eleanor Go For a Ride*, *Riding Freedom*, and many others.
(www.PamMunozRyan.com)

Written Communication

Please provide the author with all of the appropriate information in advance, including the name of the hotel, address, phone, fax, and confirmation number. Many authors and illustrators will ask you to sign a contract for their services, but if not, be certain to write out the details: date, fee, expenses, equipment needed, grade level of audiences at presentations, plus other details. If the author sends you written information regarding the school visit (perhaps a contract or letter of agreement), read it now—before you sign it—to make certain that there are no surprises. A form has been included in this chapter to help organize the essential information you will need to provide to the author.

Author Confirmation Information

School _____

School Address _____

School Phone _____ School Fax _____

Date of Author Visit and Times _____

Name/Title of Visit Coordinator _____

Work and Home Phone Numbers (Day and Evening) of Visit Coordinator

_____

Schedule of Presentations and Book Signings for the Day

_____

Presentation/Book Signing ___ Time ___ Grade Levels ___ # of Students ___

Location _____

Hotel Information

    Hotel Name _____

    Hotel Address _____

    Hotel Phone and Fax _____

    Confirmation Number _____

Transportation from the Airport _____

Name and Phone Number (Day, Evening, and Cell Phone) of the Person Picking the Author up at the Airport _____

Transportation to the Airport _____

Name and Phone Number (Day, Evening, and Cell Phone) of the Person Returning the Author to the Airport _____

Morning Pickup at the Hotel:

Day _____

Time _____

Name _____

Phone Number (Day, Evening, and Cell Phone) _____

Afternoon Return to Hotel (or Other Arrangement)

Day and Time _____

Name _____

Phone Number (Day, Evening, and Cell Phone) _____

Additional Instructions

_____

_____

_____

(If Author Is Making Own Arrangements to Get to the School) Detailed Directions to the School—Map Attached

_____

_____

_____

The Care and Feeding of an Author

Be sure to feed your author! (Yes, folks forget.) Is the author a vegetarian? It can be a long day, so how about some caffeine or sugar for the author, and be sure to provide water to soothe a dry throat. Perhaps some hot tea with lemon would be helpful. Do a little homework and find out about the author's likes and dislikes. This effort will be welcomed by your author. The worst option is to make no arrangements for lunch at all and tell the author to get lunch and come back later. (Yes, this happens.)

Alice McLerran has these suggestions for lunch: "Don't forget to have a plan for what to do when lunchtime comes. Teachers usually enjoy a chance to talk with authors, and vice versa. Don't waste time and budget whisking your author off for a restaurant lunch with just one or two teachers, though. There's more chance for contact in the teachers' lounge!

If you want to go to just a little extra trouble and make the lunch more festive, potlucks tend to work very well and are easy to organize. But you don't have to go to any extra effort unless you'd like to—the company is more important than the menu. Personally, I'm happy enough with cafeteria food, but I can't speak for every author. If you intend to send out for a deli sandwich or salad for your author, remember to check on preferences before he or she is fully involved in presentations." [Alice is the author of *Dragonfly*, *The Ghost Dance*, *Roxaboxen*, *The Mountain that Loved a Bird*, *Hugs*, and *Kisses*. (www.alicemclerran.com)]

It would be nice to let the author know what is available for lunch. We don't expect the school to pay for lunch, but if the teachers are sending out for lunch, include the author. And, have beverages on hand.

—MARYANN COCCA-LEFFLER, author and illustrator of *Missing: One Stuffed Rabbit*, *Mr. Tanen's Ties*, and *Jungle Halloween*. (www.maryanncoccaleffler.com/index.htm)

Why not make lunch at the cafeteria a special author event? Claudia Mills shared this simple and terrific idea: "One school renamed the hot lunch menu for that day in my honor, so they served 'Gus and Grandpa's Chicken Sandwich,' 'Phoebe's Fries,' and 'Dinah's Donuts.' I was thrilled." [Claudia is the author of numerous books, including the very popular *Gus and Grandpa* series. (www.childrensbookguild.org/Mills.html)]

Sometimes a few select students who would most benefit from a small group meeting will have the opportunity to meet with the author. Be certain that these students know the purpose of the author meeting and are prepared. Claudia Mills shares, "The best part of school visits for me: I love it if I can meet in a small-group format with those students who really love to read and write. I always offer to have lunch in between my presentations with a selected group of students who share my passion for books. That is what makes the whole visit worthwhile, for me."

Dan Gutman (www.dangutman.com) suggests a "Lunch with the Author," in which five to ten particularly motivated kids and Dan meet in a quiet room away from the noisy lunchroom. The inclusion of only five to ten students, he says, is deliberate; he says it doesn't work with fifteen, twenty, or thirty kids. This time together allows a small group of students to ask specific questions about writing or discuss the author's books, and the author appreciates the opportunity to meet with his or her audience in a smaller setting.

You might want to consider having an after-school event with tea and cookies or punch to bring parents, community members, or teachers together for an informal, personal time with the author. If you invite an author to dinner (which is a kind thing to do) and he or she passes, don't take it personally. Most authors are solitary creatures by nature. After spending a day with 500 kids and talking for four to five hours, they may need to be alone—to rest, decompress, or spend a few hours in their hotel room writing (deadlines are always looming). Some schools like to have a breakfast for the author before the day begins. Be sure to check with your author about this. Your author may prefer to sleep a little later, especially if he or she lives in a different time zone. If you want a casual time for the staff to meet with the author, find out what works best from your author's point of view.

A Big Thank-You

You'll want to send the author a thank-you after the visit, but it's a great idea to thank the author in person at one of the assemblies or at the end of the day. Sometimes there is a presentation of a key to the school or a proclamation. You may wish to have students make a special gift or thank-you card to present to the author to the end of the visit.

One of the nicest gifts I ever received during a school visit, was when the librarian presented me, at the end of my presentations, with two large gift bags brimming with goodies to enjoy while I was on the road. Each teacher had brought me one small item. I found a scented travel candle, a small jar of homemade jam, a box of crackers, a small tin of homemade cookies, and so on. How kind and thoughtful of them!

—MARGRIET RUURS, author of *The Power of Poems, Virtual Maniac, Emma's Egg's, A Mountain Alphabet, When We Go Camping,* and many more. (www2.junction.net/~ruurs)

Author Payment

Make arrangements to pay the author on the day of the event. If you need a social security number, an invoice, or other items to process the paperwork, find out what you need now and obtain these items in advance. If any tax information is needed to prepare the contract, send the author a self-addressed stamped envelope in which to provide it. Don't ask the author to donate the honorarium to the school, even for a very wonderful cause. (Yes, this has happened.) Be sure that the author is paid quickly and doesn't have to ask for payment or track down the coordinator of the event to receive payment. As a nicety, place the check in a thoughtful thank-you card.

Authors normally expect to be paid at the time of the visit. (Wouldn't you?) If your PTA is covering the fee, you'll have no problem: they can just write a check. But school districts often take ages to generate a check, and may require signed tax forms and even formal invoices from the author well in advance. If you're going to be facing such paperwork, make sure you understand its nature. You'll want to be sure you get things started early enough, so you can submit all needed materials in time to have payment in hand on the day of the visit.

—ALICE MCLERRAN (www.alicemclerran.com)

Host/Hostess and Introduction

Assign a host or hostess to the author for the full day who knows the teachers, classrooms, where to find equipment, and how to do other troubleshooting. Alice McLerran (www.alicemclerran.com) reminds us, "Even the most distinguished authors do need to know the location of the restroom," and Maryann Cocca-Leffler (www.maryanncoccaleffler .com/index.htm suggests that schools "have a guide to take the author from one place to another.")

At one conference, for example, student teachers were assigned to assist the authors. The student teachers were, of course, thrilled to be in this position, but had little understanding of how to assist the authors with basic questions. The student teachers couldn't answer simple questions about the purpose of the conference or where the bathroom was, nor did they know the authors' work, as they were assigned on the day of the event and had a limited background in the field of children's literature. This was the first major conference the student teachers had ever attended, and they were overwhelmed. If you are going to assign an author a host who has a limited background in order to enhance the host's professional growth (and it does have great learning potential), be sure to assign a veteran to assist the author as well, and have them work as a team.

Identify someone to introduce the author. Don't "wing it." (I remember being at a very large educational conference and cringing each time the person introducing Norman Bridwell called him Norman Birdwell.) I highly suggest that if you are the person who has coordinated the visit, that you should be the person who introduces the author. Let me explain. As a media specialist and a coordinator of library media services, I frequently organized author visits. Sometimes someone would come up to me the day of the author visit and ask if he or she could introduce the author. I would tell them "yes" and would then be disappointed in the introduction, as the person frequently didn't have enough information about the author to introduce him or her, and the introduction became a "please be quiet and listen" lecture on manners rather than an informative introduction to set the tone for the assembly. I believe if kids are prepared and your introduction quickly reminds them of the author's work and why they are there, they will pay close attention to the author because they are interested in what will be happening. If you are the person who organized the visit, it's a great opportunity for folks to see you in this position. As a coordinator of library media services, I think it was important for the school staff and community members to see me as an active participant in this event. Grab the microphone, put away your shyness or modesty, and give a brief and focused introduction for your guest.

The Physical Setup, Equipment, and Supplies

Identify and reserve an appropriate room—a quiet space with proper lighting and as few distractions of noise and foot traffic as possible—and don't place the author in front of a door. Authors bring a lot of materials with them to show students, so save wear and tear on your author and schedule all assemblies in the same room. Avoid a room that is too small and cramped, and avoid cavernous cafeterias and auditoriums. If the cafeteria must be used, try to avoid having students sit at those large tables with backless benches, and be sure that lunch tables will not be set up during the assembly. (Yes, this has happened.) If the author is using slides, videos, or overheads, be certain that the room can be darkened. Although you may show overheads in a particular room, the requirements are different for a slide presentation, so check to be absolutely certain that the room will darken enough for a slide presentation, and make adjustments if necessary. (It's disappointing, of course, to not be able to see the slide presentation because the room has so many windows that the room won't get dark enough. This is a frequent problem.)

Be sure to get a list of needed equipment and supplies from your author. Make certain that all requested audiovisual equipment will be set up and operational before the author arrives. Last-minute scavenger hunts to find working equipment just add stress to what should be an enjoyable day for everyone. Use a rolling cart for projectors to make certain that the image fits properly on the screen and can be adjusted. The screen should be large enough to accommodate the size of projection needed for the audience. Have the proper extension cords and adapters, if necessary. Most authors appreciate a large table (at least three feet by five feet) to use for their presentation items. If you are interested in videotaping or audiotaping the presentation, ask the author beforehand. Do not assume that the author will be willing to be recorded—ask permission. Your author will probably need a microphone. Find a cordless one, a lapel microphone, or one with a long cord, and make certain it works. Don't wait until the morning of the visit to see if the microphone and slide projector work. Checking on equipment before the presentation is frequently stressed by authors. On an information sheet Dan Gutman (www.dangutman.com) sends to schools he will visit, he states it this way: "PLEASE, I'm begging you, don't wait until the morning of my visit to see if the microphone and slide projector work. PLEASE! This happens over and over again, no matter how I try to stress it."

> Prior to the visit, ask the author what supplies he/she will need for the visit. Have all supplies ready when the author arrives. Make sure all equipment is in working order. (There have been many times we had to scramble for a lightbulb for a slide projector at the last minute!)

—MARYANN COCCA-LEFFLER
(www.maryanncoccaleffler.com/index.htm)

Audience

It is preferable to arrange assemblies that focus on one or two grade levels rather than on several grade levels or a wide range of grade levels. If for some reason you must have several grade levels together and your author has agreed, Brod Bagert (www.brodbagert.com) has this outstanding suggestion on how to accommodate a variety of grade levels for an assembly:

> Over the last twenty years I've done thousands of school assemblies, and if I were to isolate a single, across-the-board opportunity for improvement it would be in the composition and arrangement of the audience. Here it is.
>
> If it is at all possible, the audience should consist of no more than three grade levels, and should never skip a level. An author can do a good job for an audience of second, third, and fourth graders, but if you skip the third grade, the continuity is broken and the audience does not hold together.
>
> But what if circumstances require an audience of more than three grade levels? Just remember that an author must hold the attention of the front rows. So in a K-5 assembly with kindergarten in the front row, the author is compelled to tilt the presentation toward the kindergarten level thus losing the attention of the older children. So you must avoid seating the lower grades directly in the front of the speaker.
>
> But don't younger children need to be up front? Yes they do and there's a solution. Simply create three 'front rows' by seating the younger children in wings to the left and right of the speaker. Thus, in a K-5 presentation, you will seat kindergarten to the left of the speaker, first grade to the right of the speaker, and the rest of the audience, beginning with the second grade, in the front of the speaker.

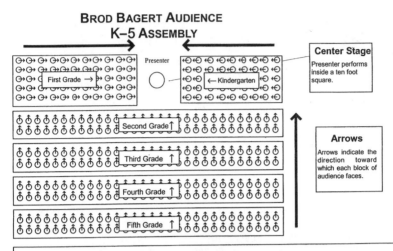

BROD BAGERT AUDIENCE
K–5 ASSEMBLY

Center Stage
Presenter performs inside a ten foot square.

Arrows
Arrows indicate the direction toward which each block of audience faces.

Space Magic

1 - Seat each child on the floor, cross-legged, with a <u>SIX INCH SPACE</u> between the knees of adjacent children.

2 - First, seat side audiences (Kindergarten and First Grade), then seat main-body audience (Second - Fifth Grades) maintaining <u>SIX INCH SPACE</u> throughout.

3 - Seat front-row children first, and maintain <u>SIX INCH SPACE</u>. (Be Obsessive!)

4 - In subsequent rows, seat each child directly behind the child in front of them, and remember to maintain WHAT? <u>SIX INCH SPACE!</u>

5 - Children tend to "squinch" together, so, until the last child is seated, teachers must be diligent to maintain <u>SIX INCH SPACE</u>.

The result is that the younger children, up front but on the side, can do all of the stuff younger children tend to do without disturbing the rest of the audience.

—BROD BAGERT [Brod does two hundred and fifty days of visitations each year. He's a "poetic Johnny Appleseed" traveling America and beyond. (www.brodbagert.com)]

Publicity

Designate one person or a committee of people who enjoy working on publicity to develop a plan. Perhaps there is a person in the district office who has experience with this and can provide assistance or offer guidance. Call the newspapers to learn deadlines and contact names for listing your event. Have the education reporter, or someone in a similar position, place the author visit on the calendar. Write a press release to submit. If a reporter is unable to attend, send an article about the visit to the newspaper after the visit. The article will provide great visibility to the community about the literacy activity. Small, local papers are more likely to be interested than larger newspapers further from the school site.

Make certain that the author event is well publicized within the school and the district. Presentations to the board of education can be effective in securing future support. After the visit or before are both appropriate times to publicize your author visit to your community. Include an article in the school newspaper providing information about the author, the author's books, and the date and time of the visit, and encourage teachers to mention the author's visit in their classroom newsletters or memos. Post the information on the school's website. Display an assortment of the author's books and information about the visit in the school library and other places where they can be seen by all students, staff, and community members. For example, make a display for the office bulletin board or display case. Many authors have commented on schools' putting up welcome signs on the school's marquee.

My Best Visits Have Been:

- Well-planned: A school representative has planned a schedule that doesn't exhaust me, along with a staff workshop or other ways to follow-up my visit. Careful travel arrangements have been made and my meals have been kindly seen to: often a potluck lunch with staff and parents helps me to meet people at the school. Some groups have even noted my favorite hot drinks and provided them for breaks!
- Well-prepared for: Students and teachers have read some of my books as well as the bio info I have sent, many have also visited my website. If book sales are desired, letters have been sent home to parents with order info, and post-it notes with names to sign are in books ready for me.
- Well-arranged physically: The setting for the sessions is attractive—a few plants added to a gym, perhaps, or books and drawings as background, along with space provided for what I bring. Arrangements for booksigning have been set up.
- Welcoming: Signs and bulletin boards with student artwork inspired by my books greet me. At times, even a pretty basket of handmade or other types of goodies is waiting for me. Parents have also been welcomed and invited to sit in on my sessions.
- Well done: Since I feel the warmth and interest in such visits, I can do my very best. I feel at ease and eager to share with those who want to hear. We all leave well satisfied with time well spent.

—CATHY SPAGNOLI (www.cathyspagnoli.com)

My Most Unforgettable Author's Visit

It was very hot in Hyderabad, South India, and I was tired after giving three assemblies, but I moved on to an army school for one last session. To help a friend, I had agreed to give a one hour workshop for 30 teachers at this school. But when I reached the gate, I was greeted by two students who cried, "Hurry, the children are waiting," as they whisked me to the headmaster's office. There, in sweet tones, he suggested we move on at once, "because the students have been sitting for a long time already."

"Students?" I asked. "I am only giving a workshop for some teachers."

"Well," he said with a sigh, "the children really wanted to hear you, too, and I just couldn't say no. But you only need to talk to them for about 1½ hours, then we'll call the teachers."

Before I could protest, I was led to a large courtyard where over 1,000 students, K–12, sat on the ground, circling a center stage. Teachers, far removed from their classes, sat happily on the outer edges of the crowd. I stumbled onto the stage under gathering monsoon clouds. Clutching the mike, I tried a few jokes to warm up and to see if my American English was understandable.

Some children listened, others talked to neighbors, teachers corrected papers, and a few birds swooped down, dropping goodies that caused more chaos. Then, in the midst of my second story, the power went off. I shouted on desperately and finished that tale when suddenly the rains came—monsoon rains that covered us in seconds, thus ending my session most effectively. Next, after a hot cup of tea, still dripping a bit, I gave the promised workshop—to over 100 teachers. At last, I left that school vowing never, ever to return there again.

—Cathy Spagnoli (www.cathyspagnoli.com)

CHAPTER FIVE

Preparing the Staff

The very best thing about a school visit is making that connection with the certain percentage of kids in the class who are seriously interested in writing. They ask brilliant questions, crack perceptive jokes, come up to me afterward, pop out of their seats when I ask "Who has thought about being a writer or artist," and otherwise do things to make their presence felt. It is a pleasure to have that brief bond, and especially to know that the effect will go on—teachers are paying attention.

—KATHLEEN KRULL

Gathering Support and Working Together

One single person acting in isolation cannot make an author's school visit successful. The best author visits are ones in which many people have had an active voice in putting it together. It is a big task for one person to handle alone, and the parts can be done better (and much more creatively!) by many people taking on different tasks. Determine the day by looking at master school and district calendars, and as soon as you have the date arranged, note it on all appropriate calendars. You don't want to have the author visit scheduled on the same day as a jog-a-thon, field day, the week of school-wide testing, or the school's book fair. (Yes, these have all happened!)

A little enthusiasm, expressed by things as simple as a welcome sign or decoration in the halls, can be the difference between a "good" author visit and a "great" one. It communicates to children that something exciting is about to happen and can lift an author to a higher level of performance.

—BROD BAGERT, a performing poet with numerous poetry collections for children and adults (www.brodbagert.com)

Enlist the support of as many people as possible when you're planning to host an author visit. I have visited schools where the Parent Teacher Organization's Literacy Committee decided to host the author visit, but failed to enlist the support of the teachers. The result has been that the children had only a vague awareness of who I am or what I do. The more aware the children are of the author and his or her work, the more they will take away from the visit. The more excited the teachers and parents are about an author visit, the more excited the children will be, the more likely they will think that reading and writing are "cool" things to do.

—LARRY DANE BRIMNER

Determine the level of interest in having an author visit the school and the willingness of your staff to prepare students for the visit. Be sure to get "buy-in" from others on your staff. Put aside your personal issues with your coworkers while the author is visiting. The author does not have a clue who your confidantes are, if you like your principal or not, or any other of the myriad interpersonal dynamics that may go on at a school site. Once, a librarian arranged a visit to a school where the author received a cool welcome and an almost antagonistic attitude from many of the teachers. They had not read any of the author's books to the children, even though there had been copies of the books distributed to share with students. The teachers barely spoke to the author in the staff room, and the author couldn't figure out what was wrong. The next day in the same school district, the author heard the scuttlebutt that the librarian was "despised" at the school and that none of the teachers wanted to participate in "that woman's" author visit. Author visits are for students and to help reinforce their love of reading and books, but this visit was about something different. You can't help thinking how petty this was and how the staff missed an opportunity.

It's essential that the staff is interested in having an author visit the school and is committed to preparing students for the visit. Get parents and staff members involved in the decision-making process and on the committee as soon as possible. Other staff members, including the principal, vice principal, other school and district administrators, and support staff should be extended a written and verbal invitation to attend a presentation. Ashley Wolff had this sound advice: "Sweet talk the janitor into doing what is needed for the day of the visit." Be sure to include the office staff—they'll probably be the first people who will be in contact with the author.

Tell your local public librarian that the author will be visiting. This is a great time to invite the librarian or librarians to attend one of the sessions. Check to see if they have books by the author in their library and perhaps whether they will order the books, as students may be requesting the books in the future. (Yes, this really does happen. It's exciting that an author visit at the school site brings students to the local library requesting books by that author.) Help your public librarians out by telling them about your author visit in advance.

Picture Books to Share

We know picture books are not just for children—adults enjoy them too. *Author's Day* by Daniel Pinkwater and Louise Borden's *The Day Eddie Met the Author* are two picture books to help you prepare your staff for an author visit, as they provide great enjoyment and insight. *Author's Day* presents a fiasco—everything that can go wrong does. It can be used as a humorous introduction to an author's visit that didn't go perfectly, and your staff can determine that your school visit will be one with far fewer wrinkles! Louise Borden's (www.louiseborden.com) book, on the other hand, portrays a positive story of an author visit and will be useful as an inspiration tool. Eddie's school is preparing to meet a "real author," and everyone has been reading the author's books. Eddie has found a part that seems as if it was written just for him, and he decides that he will ask the author the question, "How do you write books that have parts meant for me?" Imagine Eddie's disappointment when he is not called on during the assembly. The end papers of this charming book list schools Borden has visited as an author. Eddie's connection with the author's writing and her books is similar to what many of your students will experience. The book is realistic and mirrors a question from a seventh-grade student who had just read *The Strange Night Writing of Jessamine Colter* to author Cynthia DeFelice (www.cynthiadefelice.com): "How did you know to write about me?"

Informational Packet of Materials

To assist teachers in learning more about the author and the author visit and as a way of helping them prepare their students, provide them with an information packet of materials including information about the date of the visit, the author, the author's books, and the author's website preparation ideas. This communication tool is an easy way to share essential information about the author visit.

Start with a cover page that states the author's name and the date of the visit. This cover sheet should have a great graphic or be on a snazzy color of paper to capture attention and make the information look inviting and helpful. The cover sheet might include other information, if you wish, but the focus needs to capture the attention of teachers and raise expectations about the visit.

> **Worst school visit happened in Texas where an over-excited kindergartner threw up on my new boots. Her teacher carried her out, and the kid kept shouting, "But I want to see the Famous Otter, I want to see the Famous Otter." Which, of course, is what my own kids called me for years after that. Just this past spring I won the Northern California Otter Award, and it seems that somehow that little kid (who must be in her late 20s now) was prescient.**
>
> **—JANE YOLEN, author of more than 200 books, from picture books to young adult.**
> **(www.janeyolen.com)**

(Place memo on school or district letterhead with your contact information)

Date: _____
To: Visiting Teachers with (Author's Name)
From: Author Coordinator
Subject: Our Visit with (Author's Name)

I am pleased that you and your students will be visiting with (author's name) on (date) at (time). (He/She) is the author of (*Title*), (*Title*), and (*Title*). I know you and your students will have an outstanding time!

The following pages provide ideas for preparing your class for an author visit. Some of the ideas may apply to your visit with (author's name) or perhaps just give you ideas. I believe the success of an author visit depends on teachers' willingness to prepare students before the visit. Reading the author's books, doing related projects, and outlining expectations for your students during the author visit are key ingredients.

(Author's name)'s program includes a short talk, slide presentation, and some time for questions. Please prepare your students to ask (him/her) some questions.

I will be happy to work with you and assist you in any way possible. Please do not hesitate to contact me at (phone number and e-mail address).

Happy reading!

As the coordinator of a school-wide visit, it is helpful if you send a memo to each teacher as the first piece of information in the information packet. The memo will provide details about the author's visit and should be followed by the information sheet, which provides teachers with preparation ideas.

Author! Author!
Preparing Your Class for the Author's Visit: A Few Ideas

Visiting Author_____Date of Visit_____

- Read! Read! Read! Read as many of the author's books as possible to your entire class.
- Read to small and large groups of students.
- Encourage wide reading of the author's books by individual students.
- Create enthusiasm for the author's visit.
- Use the author visit to promote your reading and writing program.

- Make books inspired by the author's books.
- Have books available for students to take home and share with their family members.
- Tell parents about the author's visit.
- Send the message to parents in a class newsletter.
- Make a display in the classroom about the author and the author's books.
- Share biographical information about the author with the entire class.
- Share information about the author's website with the class.
- Have students make a welcome banner for the day of the visit.
- Have fun and be creative! Have students do art activities, music, dramatics, writing activities, puppets, posters, reader's theater, make bookmarks, and so forth to involve them in learning about the author's books.
- Help students prepare meaningful questions to ask the author.
- Discuss manners for the author's visit.

Following the memo outlining the details and the page listing a few ideas for preparing for an author visit, provide teachers with biographical information about the author, a photograph of him or her, information about the author's books, the author's website address, an order blank for the author's books, etc. The informational packet should include everything to ensure that the teacher will be informed and will have the appropriate information to share with students and students' family members.

Biographical information about the author can be obtained from the author's website, the author's publisher(s), or by using biographical information that is available from reference sources such as *Something about the Author*. Publishers often print biographical information brochures about authors or have publisher websites where information about authors is located, and don't overlook the interesting information that is sometimes found on dust jackets of an author's books.

Books and Resources Available for Staff and Students

Find out what titles your school library has by the author and how many copies are available. Consult *Books in Print*, the author, or the publisher(s) to find a list of the author's books. Order additional, multiple copies of titles for the school library now to ensure that they will be shelf-ready by the time teachers and students start preparing for the author visit. It's never too early to start this part of the preparation. You may wish to delay ordering books to sell until a later date, but order library books and classroom books for preparing your staff and students as soon as possible. Schools will need more than one copy of each book to share with students before the author's visit, and a visit generates more interest in the author's work for a long time (even years!) after the author has come and gone.

Have multiple copies in your school library for students to check out before the author's visit. Although you may wish to focus on one or two titles, get all of the books that are age- and interest-appropriate to your students. It might be the worst affront to not have any copies of the author's books in the library or any plans to purchase them. Why? For the month following a school visit, the author is the one every child in the school is dying to read. It's a crime not to have the books available and in multiple copies. In fact, the desire for students to read the author's books will last for many years at a school site as students remember the author's visit and enjoy reading and rereading the books while pointing out special items the author told them about during the assembly.

If the author has books on videotape or audiotape, purchase these or borrow them from other libraries to share with students before the author visit. Providing the author's work in other formats is an excellent way to be certain that the material can be enjoyed by students of all ability levels.

Teacher Involvement

Create an atmosphere of anticipation and excitement for your staff and your students. This may seem unnecessary to state, but it is the repeated request of authors and illustrators, so here goes: All teachers need to accompany and stay with their students for the presentation. For a multitude of reasons, this is essential and raises the importance of the visit. The author visit is an important part of the instructional day, and teachers and students will want to discuss the author's visit and respond in a variety of ways, including reading and writing. The teachers' attendance is essential to follow-up discussion and activities based on the author's visit. Some may think that it is okay to sneak out of the assembly to the workroom or lounge or think that an assembly is an additional preparation period. This sends a negative message to students as well as the guest. (It is true that teachers always have an abundance of work and little time to do it, but the author's visit is an essential part of the instructional day.)

Here's perhaps one of the biggest pet peeves and a frequent request of authors: Do not correct students' work during the presentation. This, too, sets a terrible example for students and conveys the impression that the teacher has no interest in what a visiting author might have to say. It must be tempting for the author to say, "Maybe I should come back another time, when you're not so busy? I hate to be disturbing you." Teachers are role models, yet sometimes one or two will chat during an assembly. All of these incidents tell students that they can check their attention and manners at the door. If you have teachers on your staff who might fit this description, it might be appropriate to send out a subtle little reminder. Teachers and their participation and active involvement in follow-up activities with students are a critical and essential part of the event. Additionally, the author is not responsible for the manners of students; the teachers are.

I arrived at one school to find that the library where I was to present was still in its normal configuration—a lot of round tables with chairs around them. My guidelines made it clear I needed two long tables at the end of the room and a chalkboard or some sort of easel on which to sketch or write. The number of classes scheduled for each of my sessions obviously required that ample space be cleared for students to sit on the floor in front of me. (The normal configuration was in any case inappropriate for a presentation.) I checked the clock—happily, we still had time to set up. I said cheerfully, "Well, we'd better start arranging things," and began doing so.

The librarian stared at me. "I don't do furniture," she said coldly. Fortunately, her principal arrived just then. HE "did furniture" and saw the need to do so. He and I had things ready in minutes.

—ANONYMOUS

What could be considered as an author's worst nightmare? I won't tell you who this happened to, but here's one author's worst nightmare. The author came to visit the school, and no one knew who the author was or the reason for the visit. The students hadn't read the books. The teachers didn't accompany the students to the multipurpose room for the presentations; they were all at a meeting! It seems that someone in the district had decided that hiring authors to do big school assemblies would be a way not to hire substitutes!

Black Leather Jacket

Just after *Under the Blood-Red Sun* was published, Random House took me out on a book tour that included a stop in Edmund, Oklahoma. A huge event in honor of my visit was arranged by Jeff Edwards, principal of Sequoyah Middle School, and Joe Fine, principal of Cimarron Middle School, and I'll tell you right now no one has ever done it better.

I walked into an entire school decorated in *Blue Skin of the Sea*. It was astonishing. These two men and their excellent teaching staffs went all out to welcome me. All the kids were prepared in every possible way. It was an author's dream—a school and community with a commitment to excellence.

But that's NOT the only good part. There's more. A special gift was waiting for me that neither Jeff Edwards, Joe Fine, nor I could possibly have detected. It was the gift that all who work with young people hope for, the opportunity to make contact.

After the school events—which included the most stunning array of library decorations I have ever seen, from paper fish hanging from the ceiling to detailed dioramas of scenes from *Blue Skin of the Sea*—the school and community arranged for an evening "Oklahoma Luau" in my honor. And this in the middle of winter. It was snowy and dark and cold outside, very cold. Like, what's this thin-blooded, island-raised, tropical kind of guy doing here?

Well. People came from all over to this luau. Whether out of sheer curiosity or to actually see me. I don't know. But there they were in the hundreds. All these wonderful Oklahomans at a luau (of sorts) in midwinter. I met a lot of kids and signed a lot of books. But that still wasn't the truest gift.

As I arrived with my superb Random House publicity guides, Melanie Chang and Judith Haut, I spotted a boy sitting off by himself. A boy in a black leather jacket, a new one, far too large for him. The shiny sleeves went on for another three or so inches beyond his fingertips. He'd grow into it one day, but now, as oversized as it was, it only made him seem somehow lost. He was in the seventh or eighth grade, perhaps.

I felt kind of bad that he was sitting back there so alone and went over to sit with him. I think it made his day to have the AUTHOR come sit with him, as if old friends were meeting after not seeing each other in a while. He perked up. Sat straight, smiled, even. Flopped his sleeves up on the table. He was bright, sharp, interested. We talked. I told him about how when I was a kid I didn't read and how Alex Haley's *Roots* turned me into a voracious reader at age thirty. This was very interesting news to him. We talked about *Roots*, and why it had become such a force in my life. He asked questions. Though inarticulate, this was a boy with a decent IQ.

After he and I spoke a while, I got up and mingled with the rest of the crowd. I mentioned this boy to the principal, Jeff Edwards. Jeff told me the story, that this kid was bright, but had it tough, had to struggle for the meanest of things. He lived alone with his mom, who worked a lot and was rarely home. They were struggling. The boy's father was AWOL. The boy had potential, and astonishingly to me, he had walked several miles in the dark, icy cold weather just to see me, and that this was a decision he'd made on his own. Wow.

I meandered back to the boy and talked some more, now more in line with the gravity of this connection. I asked him if he'd like to write to me. He jumped at the opportunity. Back home, I sent him a note. We decided to read *Roots* together and discuss it as we went along. I sent him a copy of the book. All mail went through the school; he'd take his letters to Jeff, and Jeff would forward them to me. I'd do the same. The boy's address changed often.

What got to me was that this boy had an inner desire to connect in some way with the world beyond the one he was given, to communicate. But he was barely literate. He said he read chapter one of *Roots*, and that it took him a while. I said that was fine. I was a slow reader, too. The idea was to live the characters' lives vicariously, though I said it in terms he could understand.

He sent me his poetry. I still have it. The topic of his writing passion was a back alley, motorcycles, knives, and guns. Gruesome, yet this was his world. To my sensibilities it bordered on hopelessness. But to him, it was simply the way it was. I urged him to write more.

After three letters he vanished. Poof! Maybe his mom moved. Maybe he lost interest. I don't know. Never will, probably. But for a time we connected. He glimpsed my world and I glimpsed his. For me it was sobering. For him it could have been anything. A dumb thing he did once. Or, perhaps, a small peek at another world.

I will never forget this boy, and I will never forget Jeff and Joe and the monumental commitment they have to the young people in their charge. Enough to mail a letter or two for a boy too rudderless to do it for himself. Edmund, Oklahoma, I hope you know how fortunate you are. I'll bet dimes to dollars you do. I know someday that boy will look back with a warmth in his heart that he may or may not understand. Maybe he won't articulate it, but will know. Oh, he will know, all right—along the way, someone cared. Wow.

—GRAHAM SALISBURY (www.grahamsalisbury.com)

CHAPTER SIX

Book Sales and Autographing

I have seen so many wonderful things that just one person insti-
gated. At every successful school visit, there was one person
who enthusiastically arranged the day and all the details.
Whether it be a classroom teacher or a media/library specialist
or sometimes even a principal, the climate of the day seems to
be held in the palm of one person's hand. That's not to say
everything always goes perfectly, because it doesn't. What im-
presses me the most is seeing the commitment that sometimes
one person at a site maintains—the commitment of passing on
the love of books to children.

—Pam Muñoz Ryan

A personal copy of the author's book, especially if it is autographed,
is a highly valued possession for children as well as adults. Selling
books is a positive and motivational experience for your students and
your staff. I hope you will want to sell the author's books. It provides
a long-lasting and tangible way of remembering the author's visit
and the celebration of reading and writing. It adds additional responsibilities to the author visit, but in future years individuals will
be rereading autographed books from their personal libraries and
students will be enjoying autographed books from the school or
classroom library.

Selling books can be accomplished in a variety of ways. Start
planning on the book selling event as soon as you've secured your

author. Order the books as soon as possible; it is never too early to order the books. Publishers often take two to three months to complete an order. It is much better for the shipment to arrive early than to arrive after the event. One of the most disappointing and frequently occurring problems that comes up with an author visit is the books not arriving in time. (Yes, this happens!) The result is disappointed students (and teachers) and a missed opportunity.

Begin by identifying the author's books, and check with the author to find out what books he or she will be discussing in depth, as that often results in more sales for that particular book. If the author does a lot of school visits, he or she may have a better understanding of what books your students will be most interested in purchasing. Seasoned authors with many school visits each year can provide sensible and accurate information about selling their books. See if your author has input into your book selling venture. Frequently, authors have the publisher contact information you will need to order books, saving you a great deal of time identifying all of the publishing information. Also, authors frequently have books with more than one publisher, so the author can often serve as a central source of information about all of his or her publishers.

When you are ordering directly from a publisher for an author's visit, the publisher frequently offers a 40 percent discount, making them an excellent source of reasonably priced books. Many schools pass the discount on to students, but others have used the selling of books to offset the total cost of the author visit and may offer the books at a smaller discount to students. Check with the publisher(s) to find out what their return policy is if you need to return books and who pays for the postage.

There are, of course, a wide variety of ways to obtain the books to sell. Local bookstores, especially children's bookstores and independent bookstores, can be especially helpful. Typically they have had experience with author visits and may be able to provide you with assistance in estimating the amount of books you wish to order, ordering the books for you, and returning unsold books after the author's visit—all this while frequently offering you a discount on the books. Their experience can be an asset to you, as they can develop a book form and perhaps even provide personnel to sell the books.

You'll want to order enough books to accommodate the demands of your students, teachers, and community members. Teachers and community members often want books for their personal libraries, but also as gifts for birthdays and holidays. This is a delightful serendipity of an author's visit—that books and the love of reading will be shared through presents to other families in other communities. Order plenty of books; if not, be prepared with a plan for those disappointed students who were unable to purchase a book. Encourage your school to purchase multiple copies of the unsold books to distribute to classrooms and the school library for students to enjoy after the author's visit—there can never be too many of the author's books available to students after the visit. After the author's visit, there will be a great demand for the books.

Here's the old debate—paper or hardback. You'll want to decide on how many paperback and hardback books to order to best meet your needs. Be sure to have both available. Obviously paperbacks are less expensive and will allow all students to own their own book, but others will want the hardback book for its long-lasting appeal.

Jerry Pallotta's Books Are Cool

A whole set of books was shipped to a school I was visiting. It was shipped UPS. There were records of the shipment and someone at the school did sign for the package. BUT the books were nowhere to be found. Every teacher and staff person looked for the missing books. Well, the guy who shipped the books for me worked at a restaurant at night. It just so happens that the clam chowder boxes from the restaurant are the exact same size as my alphabet books. Eventually the janitor got into the mix. He went to the freezer and sure enough, there were the books. The box said, "keep refrigerated" on the side. Three weeks after spending cold nights in the freezer, the books were freed and the kids finally got to enjoy them.

—JERRY PALLOTTA

Selling the Books

The books have been ordered and have arrived. Now the selling plan needs to be put firmly into place. One of the most efficient ways to facilitate the selling of books is to develop an order form to send home with students in advance of the author's visit to preorder the books. Students will be familiar with the books based on their independent reading and the books their teachers have shared with them, and the order form will serve as an outstanding publicity tool for the parents. The order form should clearly list the author's books, each book's summary, and the price (including tax) as well as provide information about the visiting author, including the date and time of the visit. Give a deadline date for money to be returned to the school to facilitate a smooth selling of the books before the visit. Send a reminder announcement later to prompt people to return their completed order forms. Preselling books allows the logistics of collecting the money to be done in advance and will simplify the day. It may be efficient to keep all of the purchased books organized by classroom for autographing and then easy distribution.

Although it is possible to sell books the day of the event, it is helpful to sell the bulk of the books before the author's visit. Sell the books at the day of the event for those teachers and students who would like an additional title, forgot their money, were absent during the preordering time, and a host of other reasons, but don't let the selling of books interrupt or overlap with the author presentation.

Autograph Sessions

If you are interested in having the author sign books, be certain to ask him or her in advance and set aside time devoted to this. If you have a relatively small amount of books to sign, you might have students wait in line, but this can be very time-consuming if there are large numbers of students or books, and it may cause loss of classroom instructional time and ultimately become frustrating to students and adults. Do you want students to stand in line for the autograph, or could the author sign books at a separate time? Most authors are willing and eager to sign books, but be certain that enough time is scheduled for this purpose. Sometimes authors are given the books to autograph the evening before in their hotel rooms. (But, be sure to clear this with the author before the visit!)

Maryann Cocca-Leffler has published more than thirty books and has visited schools in the New England area for more than fifteen years. She had this advice that has worked for her:

"Discuss the booksigning schedule in advance. If there are lots of books, you may think about shipping them to the author in advance. The author can sign the books at home and bring them to the school the day of the visit."

Develop an autograph system. To facilitate the signing of books, it works effectively to place a sticky note on each book with the name or names of the recipients clearly written and correctly spelled. Clear and correct spelling of names assists the author, prevents mistakes in the autographing, and cuts the time. (For example, is it Cathy, Cathie, Kathy, Kathie, etc.?) And, ultimately, you'll need to make a decision about how to handle students who forgot their money or those who want an autographed book after you've run out of books. One option is to make bookplates for the author to sign and then adhere them to books after they arrive, but another, more satisfying option is to provide loans to enable students to buy and have the book autographed.

It is helpful to have at least one adult sit with the author and open the books to the appropriate page for autographing. This person can also be helpful to the author if other needs arise. Sometimes, if the lines are long, it is helpful to have a person serve as a facilitator, distributing sticky notes and keeping things moving along efficiently. If the autograph time needs to be interrupted, this person can provide numbers to the remaining people in line so they can have their same place in line when autographs resume. A large table and an adult-size, comfortable chair will assist in making the autograph session more pleasant for the author.

Autographs

Children are frequently interested in obtaining an author's autograph. Signing meaningless little slips of paper that will soon be lost or misplaced, however, isn't appropriate. Also, don't put the author in the position of telling children "no" to autographs. Be sure to step up to the plate and assist the author on this one. Once a few autographs have been given, the line for autographs on paper, clothing, body parts, etc. becomes endless. One way to provide an autograph to all students, if that is desired, is to have the author sign one sheet of paper and make photocopies for each child. Another outstanding idea is to print a bookmark or an award that is signed by the author, printed in advance, and then distributed on the day of the event. Joan Bransfield Graham (www.joangraham.com) has a bookmark on her website featuring one of her poems and her signature for teachers to print out, photocopy, and distribute to students. Sometimes teachers and librarians have "author chairs" that children can sit on while reading their own work to other students. The chairs are frequently director-style chairs with canvas fabric, making a perfect spot to collect signatures from visiting authors. The chair becomes even more special and can be enjoyed for years to come. The Yellow Book Road children's bookstore, La Mesa, California, (www.yellowbookrd.com) has a fascinating wall in their store where authors and illustrators have signed autographs and made drawings for many years. Perhaps your school library or another place in the school has a perfect spot to collect autographs from visiting authors for all students to enjoy in the future.

These illustrations were made to be duplicated as bookmarks for students and can be laminated on colored paper. Courtesy of Betsy & Giulio Maestro.

I have learned to supply a master for duplication that will produce bookmarks that show my photo, signature, and the message "Writers love readers," allowing schools to give an "autographed" bookmark to every single student. I'm even more delighted when schools let students design the bookmarks for duplication. I can autograph their master when I arrive that morning, and the students have their bookmarks before I leave the school. When such bookmarks are provided, an author won't have to say "no," just explain that EVERYONE will get an autograph.

—ALICE McLERRAN

Jane Yolen (www.janeyolen.com) solved the autograph dilemma in this clever way: "I always would show up at a school half an hour early and talk to the school secretary for a minute or two about the school's character, mascots, specialties. Then I would write a verse about the school, or about reading (brand new, on the spot) and sign it. The poem would then be duplicated and given out to every single kid in school. It meant that EVERYONE had a signed poem from me. That way no one went home empty-handed."

Maryann Cocca-Leffler shared this story: "A teacher of a first grade announced that 'The AUTHOR (me) will be at the library after school to sign books.' Well, this particular first grader thought ARTHUR (of Marc Brown Fame) was going to be at the library. This poor little kid waited in line a LONG time. When he finally got to the front, he put an ARTHUR book in front of me, looked up and started crying.

'I thought ARTHUR was going to be here!' he said.

'No, I'm the AUTHOR . . . Not ARTHUR.' I told him . . . I felt so bad . . . I signed his book anyway. (Sorry, Marc.)"

About the Selling of Books at an Author's School Visit

As an author of science books for children, I have been the guest speaker at many schools across the country. Because I was a teacher, I don't do the typical program of discussing how I write. Instead, I do a performance designed to get kids interested in science. Usually my books are sold at my appearances. But there are a few places where they have not been sold and I come across a negative attitude toward the selling of books at an author's appearance that prompts this article.

There are all sorts of reasons to bring an author to a school both on the part of the children and the author. An author's appearance "makes books come alive." It shows kids that "authors are real people." Authors have enough visibility to pass as "famous" in our celebrity-crazed society, thus making the visit a special event. They are usually articulate and can present an entertaining program that reinforces interest in their books. For authors, school appearances promote their books and have a residual effect, putting their name on the map in a school for many years to come. It also gives them feedback on their readers' reactions. But, in my opinion as an educator, there is only one truly important reason to have an author come to a school: namely, to motivate kids to read. Presumably, meeting an author in person can create a demand for his or her books, particularly when the author writes, as I do, on less popular subjects. If an author excites and interests kids, the author is invariably asked, "Where can I get your books?" If the books are not at hand, the moment is lost. What baffles me is why a school that has spent some of its limited resources to bring an author to the school, obviously caring about "enrichment," does not understand how to optimize the educational experience it has created.

One argument against selling books is simply school policy: nothing is sold to kids at school, period. Any exception to the rule would somehow open a Pandora's Box of ills. In this kind of thinking, kids are characterized as avid consumers, easily manipulated by the excitement of a performance to spend money they don't have on a frivolous impulse. The schools' role is to protect them from such exploitation. A superintendent recently said to me, "If you were a rock star, the kids would want to buy your CD." I found myself in the ludicrous position of having to point out to the educator that I'm not a rock star, and it might do some good in the fight against boredom, video games and drugs to create a demand for science books along with the opportunity to fulfill it.

Another argument is, "We live in a mixed socio-economic district and we don't want to put pressure on poor kids to buy things they can't afford." My most popular books are paperbacks that can be offered in schools at a discount, priced at under $3.00. From what I hear about certain poor districts, kids have money for Nintendo, VCR's, candy bars and sometimes drugs. Why not put pressure on them to buy a book? I once signed a book for a poor child in a small village in Alaska. It was a hard cover and I didn't know he hadn't yet paid for it when I wrote his name in it. When he realized he didn't have enough money to pay for it, he was offered a less expensive book, one he could easily afford. But no. This was the one he wanted. He would bring in the money the next day. The librarian told me that there was no way his parents would give him the money to buy the book. Yet the next day he did, in fact, return for it. It was clear that this book was precious to him. Imagine! A poor child valuing a book! A small event yet one with enormous implications for the thesis that education is a way out of poverty. One reality of society is that often we think things are valuable only when we have to pay for them. And if this is yet another way to instill a value for books in children, we are remiss if we don't offer the opportunity.

Finally, there is the unstated insinuation that we authors are money-grubbers who want the royalties as part of our fee, and the schools will have no part of such greed. Personally, wearing my educator's hat, I don't care if only the $3.00 books are for sale at my appearances. Every book sold frees up the library book for a kid who truly can't afford it. The royalties will hardly amount to anything, let alone make me a rich woman. In fact, a career as a children's book author is hardly a get-rich-quick scheme. On the other hand, children's book authors are often viewed at schools as career models. If we make our living writing books, should we then be put in a position of apologizing for the fact that they are for sale?

In the real world, people earn money selling something of value, whether it's a product or a service. My fee for a day's school appearance pays for three entertaining, highly motivating programs for hundreds of children. If books for sale are not made a part of the day, the library cannot handle the demand. I become simply another entertainer for a passive audience of kids all too accustomed to being entertained. That momentary flicker of interest in reading a book quickly dies for most kids if it is not immediately reinforced. At a time when our educational systems are under fire, when students are turned off and dropping out, we can't afford to waste any opportunity to involve kids as active participants in the learning process.

—VICKI COBB is the author of numerous terrific science books for children. (www.vickicobb.com)

CHAPTER SEVEN

Checklists

The following checklists will assist you at each step of the planning. Be sure to add your own brand of enthusiasm and creativity to the mix.

Six Months to More Than a Year in Advance			
	Who Is Responsible	Due Date	Completed
❑ Get staff involved in the decision-making process	_____	_____	_____
❑ Get community members involved in the decision-making process	_____	_____	_____
❑ Get support of the entire staff for the visit	_____	_____	_____
❑ Identify author or illustrator you want to invite (See chapter 3)	_____	_____	_____
❑ Identify desired date or time frame (e.g., March or spring)	_____	_____	_____
❑ Invite the author (See chapter 3 for details)	_____	_____	_____
❑ Create your budget—be realistic!	_____	_____	_____
❑ Secure funding	_____	_____	_____
❑ Put the event on the school's calendar and the district's master calendar	_____	_____	_____
❑ Determine the author's schedule for the day	_____	_____	_____
❑ Order the author's books for the library	_____	_____	_____

- ❑ Order the author's books for classrooms
- ❑ Decide on travel arrangements
- ❑ Decide on lodging arrangements
- ❑ Provide details to author in writing
- ❑ Sign and return author's contract
- ❑ Develop a publicity plan
- ❑ Tell your public librarian about the author's visit
- ❑ Develop a book selling plan
- ❑ Develop an autograph session plan

Two to Three Months in Advance

	Who Is Responsible	Due Date	Completed
❑ Order books to be sold			
❑ Provide all staff members with informational packet of materials			
❑ Prepare staff			
❑ Provide staff members with author's website address			
❑ Make travel arrangements, if not done previously			
❑ Make hotel arrangements, if not done previously			
❑ Arrange for audiovisual and other equipment			
❑ Make banner announcing the author			
❑ Develop a display of the author's books			
❑ Create a bulletin board for the author's visit			
❑ Determine whether assistive listening devices will be needed			
❑ Submit press release to the local media			
❑ Obtain microphone			
❑ Arrange for author's supply needs			
❑ Begin to prepare your audience for the visit			
❑ Make arrangements to pay the author			

One Month in Advance			
	Who Is Responsible	Due Date	Completed
❏ Send final details to the author	_____	_____	_____
❏ Place article in school newsletter	_____	_____	_____
❏ Make certain that your book order will arrive in plenty of time	_____	_____	_____
❏ Develop an invitation to send to community members	_____	_____	_____
❏ Invite parents and other community members to attend the presentation	_____	_____	_____
❏ Invite public librarian to the presentation	_____	_____	_____
❏ Invite school board members to the presentation	_____	_____	_____
❏ Invite other people you think will enjoy the visit	_____	_____	_____
❏ Distribute author's biographical information to staff members	_____	_____	_____
❏ Identify who will introduce the author	_____	_____	_____
❏ Be certain that the principal, vice principal, other school administrators, etc. are able to attend the presentation	_____	_____	_____
❏ Display the author's books in the library, if not done previously	_____	_____	_____
❏ Develop a bulletin board publicizing the author's visit, if not done previously	_____	_____	_____
❏ Develop a book order form	_____	_____	_____
❏ Distribute the book order form	_____	_____	_____
❏ Do presales of books	_____	_____	_____
❏ Arrange to pick up author at hotel	_____	_____	_____
❏ Arrange for return of author to hotel	_____	_____	_____
❏ Identify host/hostess or guide for the day	_____	_____	_____
❏ Prepare students (see chapter 8)	_____	_____	_____

One Day to One Week Before

	Who Is Responsible	Due Date	Completed
❑ Send out second announcement for book order form	_____	_____	_____
❑ Collect book orders and money	_____	_____	_____
❑ Place "welcome author" sign on marquee	_____	_____	_____
❑ Find and retest all equipment	_____	_____	_____
❑ Send reminders home in classroom letters	_____	_____	_____
❑ Place information in school newsletter	_____	_____	_____
❑ Continue to prepare students (see chapter 8)	_____	_____	_____
❑ Check on host/hostess for author, greeting for the author at arrival, transportation to hotel, etc.	_____	_____	_____
❑ Review plans with all involved in the visit	_____	_____	_____
❑ Double-check all reservations	_____	_____	_____
❑ Get the speaking fee check ready to give to the author	_____	_____	_____
❑ Remind students that tomorrow is the big day!	_____	_____	_____
❑ Remind office staff	_____	_____	_____
❑ Collect last-minute book orders	_____	_____	_____
❑ Remind staff of the time of the visit	_____	_____	_____
❑ Encourage classes to be on time to the assembly	_____	_____	_____

Day of the Event

	Who Is Responsible	Due Date	Completed
❑ Reserve parking spot for the author (or, pick up author)	_____	_____	_____
❑ Be certain the author has water available during presentation(s)	_____	_____	_____
❑ Check equipment	_____	_____	_____
❑ Check setup of room and make adjustments	_____	_____	_____

- ❏ Take photographs, if desired _____ _____ _____
- ❏ Introduce the author to the principal
  and other staff members _____ _____ _____
- ❏ Provide lunch for the author _____ _____ _____
- ❏ Pay the speaking fee—Do it before
  the author has to ask for it! _____ _____ _____
- ❏ Final book sales _____ _____ _____
- ❏ Distribute preprinted autograph to
  students, if desired _____ _____ _____
- ❏ Add your own niceties _____ _____ _____
- ❏ Relax and have fun! Your work will
  now be rewarded! _____ _____ _____

CHAPTER EIGHT

Preparing Students for the Author's Visit

Creative teachers find ways to draw parallels and make connections between literature and whatever curricular areas they are responsible for.

—CYNTHIA DeFELICE

This is essential: Prepare students for the author visit by making certain students are familiar with the author's work. This preparation makes the difference between the author being an entertainer for a brief time or an integral part of the literacy program. This ensures that questions and other interaction with the authors will be focused on the presentations. It is a lost opportunity to not share books with students or to have numerous books for students to read independently before an author's visit. It is the simplest and most important step individual teachers can do to catapult a visit into being the most rewarding instructional activity.

Let your imagination soar! Get involved with the author's work. Make certain your students have access to many examples of the author's work and have the opportunity to respond in a variety of ways. There is a correlation between the amount of careful preparation and the amount by which each student benefits from the author's visit. But, where do you begin? Once the planning details have been taken care of, creativity and individualism can make the learning opportunities spectacular, but remember—reading the author's book is the most essential step to preparing students for a visit.

I love coming to a school and finding the halls covered with posters about my books or library shelves covered with cunning little dioramas or board games based on my books. It's so neat to see a character or a place that once existed in my head alone existing on its own— proof that ideas really do travel from one mind to other minds where they take shape and form.

Sometimes children put on plays or pantomimes based on my books—it's astounding to realize how much time and energy their teachers have put into preparing the child to enjoy my visit.

So I take this opportunity to thank all those teachers who value literature for all they do to make writers feel welcome—and to spread the joy of reading among their students.

—MARY DOWNING HAHN

Read the Author's Books

Read the author's books. Read the author's books. Read the author's books. Forego decorating, a potluck in the teacher's lounge, or a performance by the children if those activities mean taking time away from reading at least one of the author's books. It's the most important thing for making the visit meaningful to students. During an assembly when I begin talking about a particular title, I always know the classes that have read it. I can see the students' eyes light up. They'll turn and look at their teacher, nodding and smiling. They're more attentive. They have relevant questions. Sometimes they have prepared questions and they're sitting eager-eyed, holding an index card in their hands.

—PAM MUÑOZ RYAN

Best way to prepare: read the books! I went to one school once where I spoke to two fourth grades, gathered together in the library. One class had read some of my books ahead of time, and the other hadn't. It was very striking how ALL the questions came from the class that had been exposed to the books, while the other class just sat there, silent and abashed.

—CLAUDIA MILLS

Make certain that every student in the school has read (or has been heard aloud) at least one of the author's books. A book talk by the school librarians is not the same thing as actually reading the book. If the kids are not excited about the author's novels or picture books, they will not be excited about the author visit. Reading the author's work prior to the visit creates a solid foundation that the author can build on. Without this, the author will have to spend more of his or her time establishing who they are. And just about the time the kids get excited, the school buses show up to take them away.

—ROLAND SMITH

To assist you in creating your own special day, here are a plethora of ideas submitted by authors from their points of view, descriptions of their outstanding and memorable author visits. It is hoped that this cornucopia of creative activities will be a tremendous spark for your planning.

Author Visit Tips

Make sure each student is familiar with the author's work is the most important tip/rule, and I wish it were easier to enforce. It's silly for schools to spend money to bring an author to their school, yet fail to give their students any particular reason to be interested in him or her. Still, inexperienced schools sometimes seem to confuse authors with magicians or unicyclists. We're not dull people, as a rule—but we aren't performance artists.

No author should have to work a cold school! The eagerness of your students to hear what your author will have to say, and the quality of the questions students can offer, will be multiplied with the simplest and most fundamental of preparations: making each one familiar with at least something that the author writes. (I myself require that students be familiar with at least three of my books.) Reading aloud a picture book only takes minutes, and the payoff is enormous. Many picture books are actually useful for sharing with older grades. Even if an author writes only longer books, a few chapters read aloud will give a taste of the author's themes and style and tempt students to finish the book on their own.

Such preparation does more than enhance the level of anticipation—it lets your author offer easily fascinating material that would otherwise make little sense to present. Only to students who already know a book can an author explain in a straightforward way the inside story of what inspired the text, tell how an early idea was developed into the form they saw, or talk about the role of illustration in telling the story.

The more you link the author visit to what goes on in the classroom, the easier it will be to inspire your students to develop truly creative work. It's easy to design useful classroom activities related to an author's books. Carrying out some of these projects before the visit will help build the sense of excitement about the visit; doing some as follow-up can build on what the author offers.

You can also ask your author for ideas in advance! Many authors can suggest specific projects that tie in with what they have written. I already have a special handout on this topic for the schools I visit, listing ideas that encourage thinking, writing, and art. I hope soon to develop an open-ended page for my website with a richer assortment of ideas for projects.

A project created by a kindergarten teacher is one I particularly enjoy sharing. That teacher first had her students make their own illustrations for *The Mountain That Loved a Bird*—encouraging them not to copy what the artist had done, but rather to draw from their memory of the story and with their own imagination. She then chose a number of their pictures which, when pasted as a series together in logical order on a roll of paper (opening illustration on one end, closing one on the other), could help retell the story. She attached one edge of this sequence to a cardboard tube (paper-towel size did nicely), rolled up the scroll on that, and attached the other edge to a second tube. When she retold the story, slowly scrolling the illustrations one by one past the eyes of her delighted students, they were entranced. They had created a "movie!"

—Alice McLerran

Author Studies

Many teachers develop weekly or monthly author studies in which they feature an author's work while sharing biographical information as well. An author visit fits neatly into an author study and students who have had the opportunity to study other authors may have more appreciation for the visit by the "real" author. Create an author's corner featuring a collection of books by the author, biographical information, and a photo. Does the author have a website? If so, take advantage of this opportunity and have your students explore the website as well. Have a "Get to Know the Author Day" to focus on the author and the author's books.

Read 'Em and Eat

I've been to several schools (middle schools and elementary) that put on literacy events called Read and Feeds. The kids pick a visiting author's book (or several), then each class does a project based on the book. The event culminates with the visit and a lunch featuring food from the novel. During the lunch each table has a facilitator and the kids play trivia games based on the book and win prizes. It's a blast!

I went to a school last year that did a Read and Feed. They chose my novel *Sasquatch* as the theme for the visit. The entire school was decorated around the novel. They even had a live Sasquatch (played by the district superintendent dressed in a very, very hot ape costume). Now, that was a school that was prepared!

—ROLAND SMITH

Art Connection

I went to a school where the teachers had helped the kids piece together a quilt. The quilt was made of drawings (printed on fabric) that the children had made based on their reactions to my books. What a gift and what a treasure and what a tribute to the dedication of those teachers.

—ELISA KLEVEN

Scavenger Hunt

Recently, I visited a school near Rochester, New York, where the librarian had devised a clever project to encourage children to read my books. It was a Book Fact Scavenger Hunt, created by one classroom and then played by another. To make the "clues" each child chose a book, found a fact and turned it into a question. Here are some samples:

In the book *Panda*, how many countries outside China have pandas in zoos?

In the book *Ostriches and Other Flightless Birds*, why do ostriches eat small pebbles?

In the book *Killer Whales*, who is the leader of the pod?

In the book *House Sparrows Everywhere*, what do restaurants put on their roofs to discourage sparrows from roosting?

In the book *Giraffe*, how much does the giraffe's heart weigh?

—CAROLINE ARNOLD (www.geocities.com/Athens/1264)

Hallway

One of the most amazing was a middle school in Ohio that transformed the entire first and second floor hallways into the Everglades ecosystem, in connection with the book *Lostman's River*. Science, social studies, language arts, art, and music teachers were all involved, as the kids made life-sized replicas of panthers, alligators, birds, reptiles, trees, grasses, etc. and hung reports about each type of flora and fauna nearby, so you could read about every creature and life form. They created a Seminole Indian village, as well. They brought in the history of the Everglades, as well as the dangers to its future. This was education at its best!

—Cynthia DeFelice

Sports Ideas

Dan Gutman writes sports books, so he has had the whole assembly sing "Take Me Out to the Ballgame" before the program. At other times schools have held a "Million Dollar Shot" basketball free throw contest in honor of his book *The Million Dollar Shot*. If the kid makes the shot, he or she gets a prize. Dan used to give away baseballs as a prize, but he tossed one to a kid once and it hit her on the head. Visit Dan Gutman's website (www.dangutman.com) for more ideas and information about author visits.

A Warm Welcome Effort

Nim and the War Effort by Milly Lee is autobiographical and tells the story of a young girl who collects newspapers in her wagon as part of her school's newspaper collection effort for World War II. In the book, you'll notice that the family spreads newspapers on the table to read while they are eating. This is what Milly's family did when she was a child. No one was allowed to talk during the meal, and everyone read while they ate. At schools she visits, teachers have paid close attention to the details and have used the book in various ways to prepare students. Here's a story of her most memorable visit:

> As I drove up to the school, I saw a big banner "Welcome Milly Lee." There was a reserved space in the parking lot (Reserved for

Milly Lee) and a big welcome in the school office with flowers and a big badge with my name. The multipurpose room walls were covered with artwork related to *Nim and the War Effort*. They used newspapers for the background and mounted pictures about the book on them. There was a little red wagon on the stage with stacks of newspapers and one stack was wrapped with red string with a copy of *Nim and the War Effort* on it. The kids were very good, they were prepared with questions on index cards. As requested by me, there was a screen, electrical outlet, table for slide projector, and a table for the book and things I brought with me to show (for example, cigar box with Chinese school stuff, slippers from my grandmother's collection to show footbinding, autograph book with Garland Stephens' autograph, pictures of early sketches, copies of the manuscript at various stages). At lunchtime the table in the staff room was covered with newspapers, little red wagons of flowers for the centerpieces, and a delicious salad potluck lunch. A special group of student library volunteers met with me briefly at the end of the day for tea and cookies. They also sold a lot of books and had an efficient way of organizing the books by rooms with slips of paper with names. There were thank you notes and pictures from students sent after the visit. Wow! I felt like royalty.

—MILLY LEE

Favorite Author Days

I was scheduled to speak at Taft Primary School, as part of the Kern County, California Young Authors' Festival, and everyone said I should be prepared for a surprise. Since surprises can be either pleasant or horrifying, I didn't quite know what to expect. But when I walked into this little rural school, I was bowled over by the welcome. Everywhere I looked there were images from my books. Plumped construction paper raindrops dangled from the ceiling in honor of *Raindrops*, my book about the water cycle. A giant Country Bear, complete with his birthday cake costume, greeted me at a door (from *Country Bear's Surprise*). A cardboard Lightning Liz (from the book by the same name) streaked by an authentic wooden picket fence. In the auditorium, larger-than-life cardboard cutouts depicted a scene from *Elliot Fry's Good-Bye*. To put it mildly, I was overwhelmed, and very pleasantly so. Clearly, this school had studied my books in preparation for the visit. At the end of the day, however the real surprise was presented to me: a huge, handmade quilt, its squares drawn by the children and depicting scenes from their favorite books of mine. It isn't often that I'm speechless, but this was a moment when words beyond a dewy-eyed thank you evaded me.

Another visit that stands out as exemplary or above and beyond the routine was my visit to Robertsdale Elementary in Robertsdale, Alabama. This school enlisted the entire community to welcome me. A marquee in the middle of town announced my arrival: Welcome, Larry Dane Brimner, author from California! The town's florist and nursery lent the school flowers and trees and shrubs so that the auditorium could be decorated for a teddy bear's picnic. Somebody else had arranged for a white wicker table and chairs—a suitable backdrop for my programs. A group of local businessmen took me to lunch for some authentic Southern cooking at Mama Lou's. Both of these schools were standouts in my mind, and I'll long remember the enthusiasm they poured into my visits.

—LARRY DANE BRIMNER

My best visit of the year was in Dothan, Alabama. I was picked up by a limo, brought to the school, and the local television station was there. The first twenty-six kids were lined up in full costume—A through Z. A was an alligator, B was a bumble bee, C was a cat, etc. All the way to zebra. Then the 600 kids in the school lined up in the halls and we had a parade. I was led by twenty-six kids, cameras, and full costumes. What fun. A day I will never forget. The principal made the whole day an adventure.

At another school, the teachers made the Icky Bug Café. Students were dressed up in tuxedos and the Parent Teacher Organization and special students and staff were served their lunch by the student waiters. They made a menu, place mats, music, etc. It was a neat day.

Another memorable day was the day I went to a school with 300 kids. But, they had a publishing center. Each kid wrote and had bound at least three books. Think about it—there were 900 books written in anticipation of my visit. What enthusiasm on the part of the teachers! Sometimes I go to a school and they have one book written. One, but I do my best to show enthusiasm back. I don't dare tell them about the school that did 900!

—JERRY PALLOTTA (www.alphabetman.com). This is high praise because Jerry has visited more than 2,000 schools!

A school in the Bakersfield, California area hosted the most marvelous parade. The principal wore a colorful Mad Hatter chapeau and held a baton. Two girls carried a banner with wonderful artwork relating to *Splish Splash*. We marched through the playground to claps and cheers. Each first grade class had made amazing hats—daisy hats for the "Rain" poem, frog hats for "Babbling Brook," crocodile hats for "Crocodile Tears". . . one class wore shower caps, had towels around their necks and a rubber duck for "Shower." Later, over the loud speaker came the music "Splish, splash I was taking a bath . . ." and everyone starting dancing! Now that's appreciating poetry!

> —JOAN BRANSFIELD GRAHAM, poet, and author of the concrete poetry books *Splish Splash* and *Flicker Flash*. (www.joangraham.com)

The students were challenged to help the school librarian prepare for a visit by children's book author, Suse MacDonald. Their goal was to advertise Suse's visit and educate the students at Ross about Suse and her books. The children brainstormed ideas, solved problems related to preliminary preparations for the author's visit, and worked on committees. Students read and discussed the literary works of Suse MacDonald. The children formed interest groups based on one of her books, researched information, and developed presentations. Projects included written reports, posters, slide shows, videotaped plays, and sandwich boards. Students presented to other classes at Ross, to their parents, and to Suse MacDonald.

> —From SUSE MACDONALD'S website. Suse reported that this was the best project that a school did regarding one of her visits and that it took place at Betsy Ross School in Prospect Heights, Illinois. Additional information can be found on her website (www.susemacdonald) under "For Educators." Suse is the author of *Alphabatics, Look Whooo's Counting, Sea Shapes*, and *Elephants on Board*.

My best author visit ever was a week spent in Le Mans, a French city more known for its auto race than literacy endeavors. Food and accommodations in a 16th century home aside, I spent the days working with kids who'd actually read my book, were enthusiastic, and generously interacted with me in a combination of French and "American." The talks took place in classrooms, the local "mediateque," and even on the main street of a nearby village when keys could not be found to open the door to the appointed meeting place. What was most impressive was the awe the French students had for an "auteur"—any auteur. For them writing was among the highest possible callings, and a writer a person to be treated with the utmost esteem.

—KATHLEEN KARR, author of *The Great Turkey Walk*, *Many of the Family*, and *Playing with Others.*

I visited a school in El Paso once. The school was in a very poor area—most of the children were from new immigrant families. They come to kindergarten speaking no English at all, and, as the year progresses, their dedicated teachers teach them English. I only did two presentations at this school, and spoke to the third and fourth graders. But a kindergarten teacher came up to me at one point and asked me to stop by her kindergarten class if I had any time. I found the time and stopped by. This kindergarten class had drawn pictures of one of my books—*I Remember Papa*—and had these pictures displayed outside their room in the hallway. I stepped into the room, and the kids all beamed at me and, in their broken English, told me how much my story meant to them. I looked at the teacher and told her I was really surprised, because, in my opinion, *I Remember Papa* is a good story for older children, not kindergarten-aged children. She said these children were special, because they have very little, and could understand and appreciate parents sacrificing for their children. It brought tears to my eyes.

—HELEN KETTEMAN, author of *Bubba the Cowboy Prince: A Fractured Texas Tale*, *I Remember Papa*, *Mama's Way*, and others.

I recently visited a school in Cranbrook, British Columbia where the third grade teacher had studied my book *A Mountain Alphabet* with her students. They had talked about the richness of words, use of alliteration, appropriateness of subjects, etc. Then she planned an "Alphabet Fieldtrip" to a nearby historical village. You could plan this kind of trip to any place in your area: a museum or park, etc. Each student (or team) was supplied with a clipboard, paper and pencil and assigned a letter of the alphabet. They had to find objects to use in their alphabet book, in this case *A Fort Steele Alphabet*. The kids collected names of objects they saw and looked for ways to hide letters. Back in school, they worked on their sentences, choosing the best possible words and sentence arrangements. Then they designed one large illustration per letter, complete with hidden letter, and produced a gigantic alphabet book! What a great follow-up to reading my book! The project took a whole month to complete and the kids were very proud of the final result.

—MARGRIET RUURS, author of *Emma's Cold Day, Virtual Maniac, The Power of Poems*, and many others.

CHAPTER NINE

After the Visit:
Thank-Yous, Follow-Up,
and Evaluation

Thanks for coming, you made the sunshine in our eyes!

—from a letter to Robin Rector Krupp

An author visit is not over until thank-you notes are written, ac-knowledgements given, and the entire event evaluated. Where do you begin? It's important to write a thank-you note to the author. Thank yous can be from the coordinator of the visit, and students should also be encouraged to write a letter. Personal notes from teachers and students are always welcomed. Many authors value a letter that can serve as a reference for a future school visit or a comment that can be posted on the website and serve as a reference. Write your comments with that in mind—be specific and insightful about what you especially enjoyed. If you took photographs, send copies of them to the author with the thank-you note. (Only send the best few, not the ones that are blurry!) And, if the author was featured in a local newspaper, send the author a copy of the issue in which the article appeared. Sometimes authors like to feature photographs or articles on their websites.

A logical and simple writing activity is for students to write to the author. Avoid an entire classroom of students copying a scripted thank you from the board or sending half-finished or incomplete work. Send student work—only the best; if a whole class responds, don't send everything unless the author requested for you to do so.

Have students be specific about what they enjoyed the best or something that they learned.

Be certain to thank the committee members who have been helpful at each stage of the planning. If you received funding from special sources, be certain to send them a thank-you note and include a few photographs. If you received funding from a special group and you can tell them thank you in person at a meeting, arrange to do that and make that face-to-face connection with your thanks.

Letters to the Authors

"I was nervous when they said an author was coming to our school. I thought everyone who wrote books was dead. I was glad to see you weren't."

"I thought you'd be a lot younger. I guess authors get old fast."

"I thought the assembly would be boring, but it wasn't! You were funny, not some self-involved stiff."

"You're a great speaker. Maybe you should forget writing and go into politics."

—From letters written to CYNTHIA DEFELICE

"Now I know two authors. You! and Mark Twain," from Cole, Endeavour School, Bakersfield, California.

How's that for being linked with a literary name! Of course, the sparkle soon faded when I read Cole's next sentence: "So what was Mark Twain like?"

—LARRY DANE BRIMNER

I love to get letters from kids after a school visit and always collect the little gems that make my day: "My name is Steven. When I grow up I want to be an Arthur," or "Dear Mrs. Ruurs, I liked your book. The best part was the end."

—MARGRIET RUURS

More Publicity

Write a follow-up to your author visit in the school's newspaper. Include photographs and students' responses. Here's a sample newsletter article.

Sports Author Dan Gutman Visits Central School

Just about every kid loves sports, but some are reluctant to open a book. That wasn't a problem at Central School this week, where visiting author Dan Gutman used sports to get the students excited about reading and writing.

"I hated to read when I was a kid," Gutman told the fourth graders. "But around the time I was ten years old, I became a big sports fan. I wanted to know everything about sports. Reading baseball cards, magazines, and biographies of my favorite athletes made me into a reader. My mother was astonished that I grew up and became a professional writer."

Gutman, the author of *The Kid Who Ran for President*, *Honus & Me*, *Jackie & Me*, *The Million Dollar Shot*, *Ice Skating*, *Gymnastics*, and many others, entertained the students with stories of sports past and present.

First Gutman took the students through all the steps of the publishing process for fiction and nonfiction books—the idea, proposal, research, writing, rewriting, editing, gathering photos, cover design, and finally the exciting arrival of the finished book. He showed the kids his original manuscripts, early cover designs, and even read a few of the many rejection letters he has received from publishers over the years.

"I don't care how many times they turn me down," said Mr. Gutman. "I never give up."

Next, Gutman put on an amusing slide show, which he called "A Day in the Life of an Author." Finally, he answered questions from the students and their teachers.

Mr. Gutman said he was short, skinny, and a "terrible" athlete when he was a boy. "But I really loved sports," Gutman told the students, "and I was lucky that I was able to make sports part of my career when I grew up. So if there's something you really love, maybe you can make it part of your career someday too."

A good lesson for the kids. And an entertaining, and educational day at Central School. If you missed the program, you may want to visit Gutman's website at wwwdangutman.com.

Evaluation

While the author visit is fresh in your mind, consider how it went and what you might want to do next year. If your author was a novelist, perhaps next year you would like a picture book writer. If you had an author this year, perhaps you want an illustrator next year. Perhaps you want a nonfiction writer, a poet, or a writer who focuses on writing biographies, or sport stories, or any number of genres or interest areas. Now is the perfect time to reflect on this year's event and start planning for the next. Although you might be tempted, try not to compare one author's visit to another. Each author should be enjoyed and respected for his or her own unique presentation. Were the students well prepared and the facility an appropriate one? What projects did students do in preparation or follow-up to the author's visit? Were they well-executed and appropriate? If you worked through the publisher, be certain to provide the publisher with an evaluation as well as sending them a thank you for their support and assistance.

Rules, Schools (and What the Students Thought)

Realize that if the authors you are inviting are relatively new, they may be extremely nervous. I have no wish to repeat my first sweaty school visit, in Las Cruces, New Mexico. My knees shook uncontrollably, and I got numerous notes afterward from kids telling me not to say "um" so much. For me, singing lessons helped cure the stage fright, but now I am reliving the angst via my husband, Paul Brewer, a children's book artist who is making his first visits. Teachers can do small things to help, like making sure bathrooms are convenient, not expecting a performance artist, and just being aware.

—Kathleen Krull (www.kathleenkrull.com)

I was giving a presentation about animals of the Everglades at a middle school in Homestead, Florida. The classroom teacher held out a map, so the students could see what a large geographical area the Everglades really is. As the teacher lifted the map so that everyone could see it, my normally quiet four year old granddaughter, Shai (some say it should be spelled Shy because she is that way with strangers), got up from her seat in the front row, and asked if she could carry the map around the room. The teacher said yes, and Shai went from row to row holding out the map. Later that evening, while we were at a Sushi restaurant in Miami, Shai behaved badly, saying "You won't do what you're 'posed to do." When I asked what that was, she gestured to all of the people in the restaurant. I asked what she meant, and she said, "Papa, go ahead and do it!" I said, "Do what?" She burst into tears.

When I finally calmed her down I discovered that she wanted me to continue my Everglades talk for the people in the restaurant, and she, of course, wanted to carry the map around, too. I had to explain the difference between classrooms and restaurants, students and diners. Shai still accompanies us whenever we can bring her along, and once while one of my programs was being televised, Shai caught the eye of the cameraman and the final footage shown on the news that evening showed Shai, not me. The girl who wouldn't speak to strangers has become quite a storyteller. One of the greatest perks her storytelling grandfather could ever ask for.

—Gerald Hausman

I write books and do school visits for several reasons—one is that it's very important to me that kids read. Another is that it's also important to me that children use their imaginations. When I write my books and do my presentations, these are the things I talk about and stress. I've gotten so many letters from children—and teachers too—after school visits—saying things like thanks for coming, they loved my presentation, and storytelling, they love my books—all of these things. Here are a few that I particularly love.

"I loved your stories. They are funny. You should be a comedienne."

"I love your stories. My favorite is *I Remember Papa*, because my grandpa died and I miss him."

"Thank you for telling us how to write stories. I am excited to write some stories now."

And maybe my all-time favorite: "I love your books. They make me imagine things."

—Helen Ketteman

Your books are better than a roller-coaster!

—second grader, Antelope, California, to Robin Rector Krupp
(rrkrupp@hotmail.com)

After-Visit Checklist

	Who Is Responsible	Due Date	Completed
❏ Write a thank-you to the author	⎯⎯	⎯⎯	⎯⎯
❏ Have students write thank-you notes to the author	⎯⎯	⎯⎯	⎯⎯
❏ Write thank-you notes to committee members	⎯⎯	⎯⎯	⎯⎯
❏ Send thank-you notes to all other collaborating groups	⎯⎯	⎯⎯	⎯⎯
❏ Evaluate the author visit	⎯⎯	⎯⎯	⎯⎯
❏ Place an article about the author visit in the school newspaper	⎯⎯	⎯⎯	⎯⎯
❏ Return unsold books to the book seller or publisher	⎯⎯	⎯⎯	⎯⎯
❏ Start student projects based on the author's work	⎯⎯	⎯⎯	⎯⎯
❏ Begin planning for your next author event!	⎯⎯	⎯⎯	⎯⎯

Author Resources

Here is a list of recommended books and helpful contact information for some excellent authors. Many of their websites have sections that tell specifics about organizing an author visit with them and will provide you with additional contact information.

Caroline Arnold

www.geocities.com/Athens/1264; e-mail: csarnoldbooks@yahoo.com
Australian Animals. New York: HarperCollins, 2000.
Did You Hear That?: Animals with Superhearing. Watertown, MA: Charles-
bridge, 2001.
Dinosaurs with Feathers. New York: Clarion, 2001.
Easter Island. New York: Clarion, 2000.
Giant Shark. New York: Clarion, 2000.

Louise Borden

www.louiseborden.com
The Day Eddie Met the Author. Illustrated by Adam Gustavson. New York:
Margaret K. McElderry Books, 2001.

Brod Bagert

www.brodbagert.com; e-mail: julhouse@aol.com; Juliahouse Tours: Phone/
Fax: (800) 999-9652

Chicken Socks and Other Contagious Poems. Illustrated by Tim Ellis. Honesdale, PA: Boyds Mills Press, 1994.

Elephant Games and Other Playful Poems to Perform. Illustrated by Tim Ellis. Honesdale, PA: Boyds Mills Press, 1995.

The Gooch Machine: Poems for Children to Perform. Illustrated by Tim Ellis. Honesdale, PA: Boyds Mills Press, 1997.

Let Me Be The Boss and Other Poems for Kids to Perform. Illustrated by Tim Ellis. Honesdale, PA: Boyds Mills Press, 1992.

Rainbows, Head Lice, and Pea-Green Tile: Poems in the Voice of the Classroom Teacher. Illustrated by Kim Doner. Gainesville, FL: Maupin House, 1999.

Paul Brewer

e-mail: pbrewer@san.rr.com

Krull, Kathleen. *Clip, Clip, Clip: Three Stories about Hair*. Illustrated by Paul Brewer. New York: Holiday House, 2001.

Seuling, Barbara. *Oh No, It's Robert*. Illustrated by Paul Brewer. Chicago, IL: Front Street, 1999.

Seuling, Barbara. *Robert and the Great Pepperoni*. Illustrated by Paul Brewer. Chicago, IL: Front Street, 2001.

Larry Dane Brimner

www.brimner.com; e-mail: ldb@brimner.com

Angel Island. New York: Children's Press, 2001.

Cat on Wheels. Illustrated by Mary Peterson. Honesdale, PA: Boyd Mills Press, 2000.

Elliot Fry's Good-Bye. Illustrated by Eugenie Fernandes. Honesdale, PA: Boyd Mills Press, 1998.

The Littlest Wolf. Illustrated by Jose Aruego and Ariane Dewey. New York: HarperCollins, 2002.

Merry Christmas, Old Armadillo. Illustrated by Dominic Catalano. Honesdale, PA: Boyd Mills Press, 1995.

Nana's Hog. Illustrated by Susan Miller. New York: Children's Press, 1998.

Mary Casanova

www.marycasanova.com; e-mail: mary@marycasanova.com

The Hunter: A Chinese Folktale. Illustrated by Ed Young. New York: Atheneum, 2000.

Moose Tracks. New York: Hyperion, 1995.

Riot. New York: Hyperion, 1996.

Stealing Thunder. New York: Hyperion, 1999.
Wolf Shadows. Illustrated by Dan Brown. New York: Hyperion, 1997.

Andrew Clements

www.eduplace.com/kids/hmr/mtai/clements.html and www.frindle.com
Double Trouble in Walla Walla. Illustrated by Sal Murdocca. Brookfield, CT: Millbrook, 1997.
Frindle. New York: Simon and Schuster, 1996.
The Landry News. New York: Simon and Schuster, 1999.

Vicki Cobb

www.vickicobb.com
Perk Up Your Ears: Discover Your Sense of Hearing. Illustrated by Cynthia C. Lewis. Brookfield, CT: Millbrook, 2001.
See for Yourself: More than 100 Experiments for Science Fairs and Projects. Illustrated by Dave Klug. New York: Scholastic, 2001.
Squirts and Spurts: Science Fun with Water. Illustrated by Steve Haefele. Brookfield, CT: Millbrook, 2000.
This Place Is Cold (Imagine Living Here). Illustrated by Barbara Lavallee. New York: Walker, 1991.
You Gotta Try This! Absolutely Irresistible Science. Illustrated by True Kelley. New York: Morrow, 1999.

Maryann Cocca-Leffler

www.maryanncoccaleffler.com; e-mail: MCLeffler@aol.com
Bus Route to Boston. Honesdale, PA: Boyds Mills, 2000.
Clams All Year. Honesdale, PA: Boyds Mills, 1996.
Jungle Halloween. Morton Grove, IL: Albert Whitman, 2000.
Missing: One Stuffed Rabbit. Morton Grove, IL: Albert Whitman, 1998.
Mr. Tanen's Ties. Morton Grove, IL: Albert Whitman, 1999.

Sneed B. Collard III

www.author-illust-source.com/sneedbcollard.htm
Animal Dads. Illustrated by Steve Jenkins. Boston, MA: Houghton Mifflin, 1997.
Butterfly Count. Illustrated by Paul Kratter. New York: Holiday House, 2002.
The Forest in the Clouds. Illustrated by Michael Rothman. Watertown, MA: Charlesbridge, 2000.

Leaving Home. Illustrated by Joan Dunning. Boston, MA: Houghton Mifflin, 2002.
Making Animal Babies. Illustrated by Steve Jenkins. Boston, MA: Houghton Mifflin, 2000.

Katie Davis

www.katiedavis.com; e-mail: katiedavis@katiedavis.com
I Hate to Go to Bed! San Diego, CA: Harcourt, 1999.
Party Animals. San Diego, CA: Harcourt, 2002.
Scared Stiff. San Diego, CA: Harcourt, 2001.
Who Hoots? San Diego, CA: Harcourt, 2000.
Who Hops? San Diego, CA: Harcourt, 1998.

Cynthia DeFelice

www.cynthiadefelice.com; e-mail: cyndefelice@yahoo.com
Casey in the Bath. Illustrated by Chris L. Demarest. New York: Farrar, Straus and Giroux, 1996.
Death at Devil's Bridge. New York: Farrar, Straus and Giroux, 2000.
Nowhere to Call Home. New York: Farrar, Straus and Giroux, 1999.
Weasel. New York: Atheneum, 1990.
The Strange Night Writing of Jassamine Colter. New York: Atheneum, 1988.

Betsy Duffey

www.BetsyDuffey.com
Cody's Secret Admirer. New York: Viking, 1998.
Fur-Ever Yours, Booker Jones. New York: Viking, 2001.
How to Be Cool in the Third Grade. New York: Viking, 1993.
Utterly Yours, Booker Jones. New York: Viking, 1995.
Duffey, Betsy, Betsy Byars, and Laurie Myers. *My Dog, My Hero.* New York: Holt, 2000.

Jean Ferris

e-mail: jferris1@aol.com
Across the Grain. New York: Farrar, Straus and Giroux, 1993.
Bad. New York: Farrar, Straus and Giroux, 1998.
Eight Seconds. New York: Farrar, Straus and Giroux, 2000.
Love among the Walnuts: Or How I Saved My Entire Family From Being Poisoned. San Diego, CA: Harcourt, 1998.
Of Sound Mind. New York: Farrar, Straus and Giroux, 2001.

Edith Hope Fine

www.grammarpatrol.com
Gary Paulsen: Author and Wilderness Adventurer. Berkeley Heights, NJ: Enslow, 2000.
Fine, Edith Hope, and Judith P. Josephson. *More Nitty-Gritty Grammar: Another Not-So-Serious Guide to Clear Communication.* Berkeley, CA: Ten Speed Press, 2001.
Fine, Edith Hope, and Judith P. Josephson. *Nitty-Gritty Grammar: A Not-So-Serious Guide to Clear Communication.* Berkeley, CA: Ten Speed Press, 1998.
Under the Lemon Moon. Illustrated by René King Moreno. New York: Lee & Low, 1999.

Mary Ann Fraser

www.maryannfraser.com; e-mail: maryafraser@aol.com
In Search of the Grand Canyon: Down the Colorado with John Wesley Powell. New York: Holt, 1995.
Ten Mile Day and the Building of the Transcontinental Railroad. New York: Holt, 1993.
Vicksburg: The Battle that Won the Civil War. New York: Holt, 1999.
Where Are the Night Animals? New York: HarperCollins, 1998.
Hawes, Judy. *Why Frogs Are Wet.* Illustrated by Mary Ann Fraser. New York: HarperCollins, 2000.

Evelyn Gallardo

www.evegallardo.com; e-mail: evegal22@aol.com
Among the Orangutans: The Birute Galdikas Story. San Francisco, CA: Chronicle, 1993.

Joan Bransfield Graham

www.joangraham
Flicker Flash. Illustrated by Nancy Davis. New York: Houghton Mifflin, 1999.
Splish Splash. Illustrated by Steven Scott. New York: Houghton Mifflin, 1994.

Dan Gutman

www.dangutman.com; e-mail: Dangut@aol.com
Babe and Me: A Baseball Card Adventure. New York: Avon, 2000.
Honus and Me: A Baseball Card Adventure. New York: Avon, 1997.
Jackie and Me: A Baseball Card Adventure. New York: Avon, 1999.

The Kid Who Ran for President. New York: Scholastic, 1996.
The Million Dollar Kick. New York: Hyperion, 2001.

Mary Downing Hahn

www.childrensbookguild.org/hahn.html; e-mail: MDH1293@aol.com
Anna All Year Round. New York: Clarion, 1999.
Anna on the Farm. New York: Clarion, 2001.
December Stillness. New York: Clarion, 1988.
Time for Andrew: A Ghost Story. New York: Clarion, 1994.
Wait Till Helen Comes. New York: Clarion, 1986.

Gerald Hausman

www.geraldhausman.com; e-mail: ghausman@compuserve.com
Doctor Bird: Three Jamaican Lookin' Up Tales. Illustrated by Ashley Wolff. New York: Philomel, 1998.
The Story of Blue Elk. Illustrated by Kristina Rodanas. Boston, MA: Houghton Mifflin, 1998.
Tom Cringle: Battle on the High Seas. New York: Simon and Schuster, 2000.
Tom Cringle: The Pirate and the Patriot. New York: Simon and Schuster, 2001.
Hausman, Gerald, and Uton Hinds. *The Jacob Ladder*. New York: Orchard, 2001.

Kathryn Hewitt

e-mail: khewitt@gateway.net
Bunting, Eve. *Sunflower House*. Illustrated by Kathryn Hewitt. San Diego, CA: Harcourt, 1996.
Cullen, Lynn. *Godiva*. Illustrated by Kathryn Hewitt. New York: Golden Books, 2001.
Krull, Kathleen. *Lives of the Artists: Masterpieces, Messes (and What the Neighbors Thought)*. Illustrated by Kathryn Hewitt. San Diego, CA: Harcourt, 1995.
Krull, Kathleen. *Lives of the Extraordinary Women: Rulers, Rebels (and What the Neighbors Thought)*. Illustrated by Kathryn Hewitt. San Diego, CA: Harcourt, 2000.
Robertson, Bruce. *Marguerite Makes a Book*. Illustrated by Kathryn Hewitt. Los Angeles, CA: J. Paul Getty Museum, 1999.

Kathleen Karr

www.childrensbookguild.org/kathleenkarr.html; e-mail: Karr@bellatlantic.net
The Boxer. New York: Farrar, Straus and Giroux, 2000.

The Great Turkey Walk. New York: Farrar, Straus and Giroux, 1998.
It Happened in the White House: Extraordinary Tales from America's Most Famous Home. New York: Hyperion, 2000.
Man of the Family. New York: Farrar, Straus and Giroux, 1999.
Playing with Fire. New York: Farrar, Straus and Giroux, 2001.

Helen Ketteman

www.flash.net/ ~ helenket/; e-mail: helenket@flash.net
Armadillo Tattletale. Illustrated by Keith Graves. New York: Scholastic, 2000.
Bubba the Cowboy Prince: A Fractured Texas Tale. Illustrated by James Warhola. New York: Scholastic, 1997.
I Remember Papa. Illustrated by Greg Shed. New York: Dial, 1998.
Mama's Way. Illustrated by Mary Whyte. New York: Dial, 2001.
Shoeshine Whittaker. Illustrated by Scott Goto. New York: Walker and Co., 1997.

Elisa Kleven

www.elisakleven.com; e-mail: EKleven@aol.com
Hooray, A Piñata! New York: Dutton, 1996.
The Lion and the Little Red Bird. New York: Dutton, 1992.
The Paper Princess. New York: Dutton, 1994.
The Puddle Pail. New York: Dutton, 1997.
Sun Bread. New York: Dutton, 2001.

Kate Klise

KateKlise@aol.com
Letters from Camp. Illustrated by M. Sarah Klise. New York: Avon Camelot, 1999.
Regarding the Fountain. Illustrated by M. Sarah Klise. New York: Avon Books, 1998.
Trial by Journal. Illustrated by M. Sarah Klise. New York: HarperCollins, 2001.

M. Sarah Klise

msklise@pacbell.net
Klise, Kate. *Letters from Camp*. Illustrated by M. Sarah Klise. New York: Avon Camelot, 1999.
Klise, Kate. *Regarding the Fountain*. Illustrated by M. Sarah Klise. New York: Avon Books, 1998.

Klise, Kate. *Trial by Journal*. Illustrated by M. Sarah Klise. New York: Harper-Collins, 2001.

Kathleen Krull

www.kathleenkrull.com
Gonna Sing My Head Off: American Folk Songs for Children. Illustrated by Allen Garns. New York: Knopf, 1992.
A Kid's Guide to America's Bill of Rights: Curfews, Censorship, and the 100-Pound Giant. New York: Avon, 1999.
Lives of the Artists: Masterpieces, Messes (and What the Neighbors Thought). Illustrated by Kathryn Hewitt. San Diego, CA: Harcourt, 1995.
Lives of the Musicians: Good Times, Bad Times (and What the Neighbors Thought). Illustrated by Kathryn Hewitt. San Diego, CA: Harcourt, 1993.
Lives of the Writers: Comedies, Tragedies (and What the Neighbors Thought). Illustrated by Kathryn Hewitt. San Diego, CA: Harcourt, 1994.
Wilma Unlimited: How Wilma Rudolph Became the World's Fastest Woman. Illustrated by David Diaz. San Diego, CA: Harcourt, 1996.

Robin Rector Krupp

e-mail: rrkrupp@hotmail.com
Let's Go Traveling. New York: Morrow, 1992.
Let's Go Traveling in Mexico. New York: Morrow, 1996.
Krupp, E. C. *The Big Dipper and You*. Illustrated by Robin Rector Krupp. New York: HarperCollins, 1999.
Krupp, E. C. *The Rainbow and You*. Illustrated by Robin Rector Krupp. New York: HarperCollins, 2000.

Milly Lee

e-mail: nimlee@aol.com
Earthquake. Illustrated by Yangsook Choi. New York: Farrar, Straus and Giroux, 2000.
Nim and the War Effort. Illustrated by Yangsook Choi. New York: Farrar, Straus and Giroux, 1997.

Suse MacDonald

www.susemacdonald.com
Alphabatics. New York: Simon and Schuster, 1986.
Elephants on Board. San Diego, CA: Harcourt, 1999.

Look Whooo's Counting. New York: Scholastic, 2000.
Sea Shapes. San Diego, CA: Harcourt, 1994.

Alice McLerran

www.alicemclerran.com
Dragonfly. Spring, TX: Absey and Co., 2000.
The Ghost Dance. Illustrated by Paul Morin. New York: Clarion, 1995.
The Legacy of Roxaboxen: A Collection of Voices. Spring, TX: Absey and Co., 1998.
The Mountain That Loved a Bird. Illustrated by Eric Carle. New York: Simon and Schuster, 1985.
Roxaboxen. Illustrated by Barbara Cooney. New York: Lothrop, 1991.

Bruce McMillan

www.brucemcmillan.com; e-mail: bruce@brucemcmillan.com
Eating Fractions. New York: Scholastic, 1991.
Growing Colors. New York: Lothrop, 1988.
Mouse Views: What the Class Pet Saw. New York: Holiday House, 1993.
Puffins Climb, Penguins Rhyme. San Diego, CA: Gulliver, 1995.
The Weather Sky. New York: Farrar, Straus and Giroux, 1991.

Betsy and Giulio Maestro

www.maestrobooks.com
Maestro, Betsy. *The New Americans: Colonial Times, 1620–1689.* Illustrated by Giulio Maestro. New York: HarperCollins, 1998.
——— . *The Story of Clocks and Calendars: Marking a Millennium.* Illustrated by Giulio Maestro. New York: HarperCollins, 1995.
——— . *The Story of Money.* Illustrated by Giulio Maestro. New York: Clarion, 1993.
——— . *Taxi: A Book of City Words.* Illustrated by Giulio Maestro. New York: Clarion, 1989.
——— . *The Voice of the People: American Democracy in Action.* Illustrated by Giulio Maestro. New York: HarperCollins, 1996.

Julie Mammano

www.childrensauthorsnetwork.com/julie_mammano.htm; e-mail: waycoolrhinos @juno.com
Rhinos Who Play Soccer. San Francisco, CA: Chronicle, 2001.
Rhinos Who Skateboard. San Francisco, CA: Chronicle, 1999.

Rhinos Who Snowboard. San Francisco, CA: Chronicle, 1997.
Rhinos Who Surf. San Francisco, CA: Chronicle, 1996.

Michelle Markel

home.earthlink.net/ ~ cohen_markel/; e-mail: cohen_markel@earthlink.net
Cornhusk, Silk and Wishbones: A Book of Dolls from Around the World. Boston, MA: Houghton Mifflin, 2000.
Gracias, Rosa. Illustrated by Diane Paterson. Morton Grove, IL: Albert Whitman, 1985.

Claudia Mills

www.childrensbookguild.org/Mills.html
Gus and Grandpa and Show-and-Tell. Illustrated by Catherine Stock. New York: Farrar, Straus and Giroux, 2000.
Gus and Grandpa at Basketball. Illustrated by Catherine Stock. New York: Farrar, Straus and Giroux, 2001.
Lizzie at Last. New York: Farrar, Straus and Giroux, 2000.
7 x 9 = Trouble. Illustrated by G. Brian Karas. New York: Farrar, Straus and Giroux, 2002.
Standing Up to Mr. O. New York: Farrar, Straus and Giroux, 1998.

Alexis O'Neill

www.alexisoneill.com; e-mail: AlexisInCA@aol.com
Estela's Swap. New York: Lee & Low, 2002.
Loud Emily. New York: Simon and Schuster, 1998.
The Recess Queen. New York: Scholastic, 2002.

Jerry Pallotta

www.alphabetman.com
Dory Story. Illustrated by David Biedrzycki. Watertown, MA: Charlesbridge, 2000.
The Icky Bug Alphabet Book. Illustrated by Ralph Masiello. Watertown, MA: Charlesbridge, 1990.
The Icky Bug Counting Book. Illustrated by Ralph Masiello. Watertown, MA: Charlesbridge, 1992.
Freshwater Alphabet Book. Illustrated by David Biedrzycki. Watertown, MA: Charlesbridge, 1996.
The Ocean Alphabet Book. Illustrated by Frank Mazzola. Watertown, MA: Charlesbridge, 1990.

Daniel Pinkwater

www.pinkwater.com
Author's Day. New York: Macmillan, 1993.

Joan Singleton Prestine

www.JoanPrestine.com
It's Hard to Share My Teacher. Torrance, CA: Fearon Teacher Aids, 1994.
Mom and Dad Break Up. (Kids Have Feelings Too Series.) Torrance, CA: Fearon Teacher Aids, 1996.

Margriet Ruurs

www2.junction.net/ ~ ruurs; e-mail: ruurs@junction.net
Emma's Cold Day. North York, Ontario, Canada: Stoddard Kids, 2001.
A Mountain Alphabet. Illustrated by Andrew Kiss. Toronto, Ontario, Canada: Tundra Books, 1996.
The Power of Poems: Teaching the Joy of Writing Poetry. Gainesville, FL: Maupin House, 2000.
Virtual Maniac: Silly and Serious Poems for Kids. Gainesville, FL: Maupin House, 2000.
When We Go Camping. Illustrated by Andrew Kiss. Toronto, Ontario, Canada: Tundra Books, 2001.

Pam Muñoz Ryan

www.PamMunozRyan.com
Amelia and Eleanor Go for a Ride. Illustrated by Brian Selznick. New York: Scholastic, 1999.
Esperanza Rising. New York: Scholastic, 2000.
The Flag We Love. Illustrated by Ralph Masiello. Watertown, MA: Charlesbridge, 1996.
Mice and Beans. Illustrated by Joe Cepeda. New York: Scholastic, 2001.
Riding Freedom. New York: Scholastic, 1998.
When Marian Sang. Illustrated by Brian Selznick. New York: Scholastic, 2002.

Graham Salisbury

www.grahamsalisbury.com
Blue Skin of the Sea. New York: Yearling, 1998.
Island Boyz. New York: Delacorte Press, 2002.
Jungle Dogs. New York: Delacorte Press, 1998.

Shark Bait. New York: Bantam, 1997.
Under the Blood-Red Sun. New York: Yearling Books, 1995.

Barney Saltzberg

www.barneysaltzberg.com; e-mail: inkless@aol.com
Animal Kisses: A Touch and Feel Book. San Diego, CA: Harcourt, 2000.
The Problem with Pumpkins: A Hip and Hop Story. San Diego, CA: Harcourt, 2001.
The Soccer Mom from Outer Space. New York: Crown, 2000.
Sierra, Judy. *There's a Zoo in Room 22.* Illustrated by Barney Saltzberg. San Diego, CA: Harcourt, 2000.

Roland Smith

www.rolandsmith.com; e-mail: rolands648@aol.com
The Captain's Dog: My Journey with the Lewis and Clark Tribe. San Diego, CA: Gulliver, 1999.
Jaguar. New York: Hyperion, 1997.
Sasquatch. New York: Hyperion, 1998.
Thunder Cave. New York, Hyperion, 1995.
Zach's Lie. New York: Hyperion, 2000.

Cathy Spagnoli

www.cathyspagnoli.com
Asian Tales and Tellers. Little Rock, AR: August House, 1998.
Judge Rabbit and the Tree Spirit: A Folktale from Cambodia. Illustrated by Nancy Horn. San Francisco, CA: Children's Book Press, 1991.
Nine-In-One Grr! Grr! Illustrated by Nancy Horn. San Francisco, CA: Children's Book Press, 1989.
Terrific Trickster Tales from Asia. Fort Atkinson, WI: Highsmith Press, 2001.
A Treasury of Asian Stories and Activities for Schools and Libraries. Fort Atkinson, WI: Upstart Books, 1998.

April Wayland

www.aprilwayland.com
It's Not My Turn to Look For Grandma! Illustrated by George Booth. New York: Knopf, 1995.
Poetry Is My Underwear. New York: Knopf, 2002.

Ashley Wolff

www.ashleywolff.com

Stella and Roy Go Camping. New York: Dutton, 1999.

Slate, Josef. *Miss Bindergarten Celebrates the 100th Day of Kindergarten.* Illustrated by Ashley Wolff. New York: Dutton, 1998.

Slate, Josef. *Miss Bindergarten Gets Ready for Kindergarten.* Illustrated by Ashley Wolff. New York: Dutton, 1996.

Slate, Josef. *Miss Bindergarten Stays Home from Kindergarten.* Illustrated by Ashley Wolff. New York: Dutton, 2000.

Slate, Josef. *Miss Bindergarten Takes a Field Trip with Kindergarten.* Illustrated by Ashley Wolff. New York: Dutton, 2000.

Janet S. Wong

www.janetwong.com

Behind the Wheel: Poems about Driving. New York: Simon and Schuster, 1999.

BUZZ. Illustrated by Margaret Chodos-Irvine. San Diego, CA: Harcourt, 2000.

Good Luck Gold. New York: Simon and Schuster, 1994.

Grump. Illustrated by John Wallace. New York: Simon and Schuster, 2001.

This Time Next Year. Illustrated by Yangsook Choi. New York: Farrar, Straus and Giroux, 2000.

Jane Yolen

www.janeyolen.com

Encounter. Illustrated by David Shannon. San Diego, CA: Harcourt, 1992.

How Do Dinosaurs Say Good Night? Illustrated by Mark Teague. New York: Scholastic, 2000.

Not One Damsel in Distress: World Folktales for Strong Girls. San Diego, CA: Harcourt, 2000.

Owl Moon. Illustrated by John Schoenherr. New York: Philomel, 1987.

Yolen, Jane, and Bruce Coville. *Armageddon Summer.* San Diego, CA: Harcourt, 1998.

Website Resources

Here are some websites that may be helpful to you in identifying an appropriate author for your audience.

www.ucalgary.ca/ ~ dkbrown/authors.html

This is from *Children's Literature Web Guide*. The web guide gathers and categorizes Internet resources as they relate to books for children and young adults. It is under the direction of David K. Brown, Doucette Library of Teaching Resources, University of Calgary. You will find websites listed alphabetically by last name, including authors' personal websites and websites that are maintained by "fans, scholars, or readers." A bouquet of flowers indicates an Internet resource that they feel is particularly valuable. And, they remind readers, "if you can't find anything about the author online, you may still be able to find something in a library." Some of the authors are willing to visit schools, and the website is informative about a variety of issues related to children's literature.

www.author-illustr-source.com

This website lists published authors or illustrators who make "school visits to enrich curriculum at all grade levels of public and private schools or for professional development workshops and seminars." You can browse the listings alphabetically and narrow your browsing by geographically sorted regions such as Northeast, Mid-Atlantic, South, Midwest, West, or Pacific; they also have a listing for Africa. The authors and illustrators are listed alphabetically, and each listing provides biographical information, published books, description(s) of the presentation(s) made, number of presentations preferred, audiovisual equipment required, the fee, and a way to contact the author. Authors pay an annual fee to be listed at this website. For more information contact: Paul Oughton, Author Illustrator Source, 1220 Gainesway Dr., Lexington, KY 40517, phone (859) 272-9828.

www.authorsillustrators.com

Every author listed on this website wants to speak in schools and has experience doing so. Contact the authors or illustrators and they will provide you with detailed information about their programs, prices, and current references. You arrange all the logistics of the visit directly with the author or illustrator. Their list of authors and illustrators includes Robert F. Baldwin, Larry Dane Brimner, Greg Brown, Marguerite W. Davol, Ann Fearrington, Lisa Funari-Willever, Evelyn Gallardo, Mordicai Gerstein, Marilyn Gould, David Greenbert, Steve Isham, Christine Petrell Kallevig, Daniel Lane, Amy MacDonald, Betsy and Giulio Maestro, Cynthia Mercati, Herman Parish, David Patneaude, Laurence Pringle, Peter and Connie Roop, Kathy Ross, Michael Elsohn Ross, Irene Smalls, Richard Lynn Stack, and Sandra Warren. For a complete catalog contact: Authors and Illustrators Who Visit Schools, 7327 SW Barnes Rd., PMB 623, Portland, OR 97235, phone: (503) 297-8136, fax: (503) 297-8141, e-mail: AIVS@authorillustrators.com.

www.californiareads.org

A *Taste of Literacy* is only available directly through the California Reading Association. Compiled and edited by Dr. Helen Foster James, it includes 124 California children's book authors' and illustrators' recipes, literacy memories, and their contact information. Authors and illustrators include Alma Flor Ada, Eve Bunting, Janell Cannon, Joe Cepeda, Cynthia Chin-Lee, Karen English, Kristine O'Connell George, Nikki Grimes, Monica Gunning, Tony Johnston, Laura Numeroff, Peggy Rathmann, David Shannon, Judy Sierra, Erica Silverman, Natasha Wing, and many more. Particularly helpful if you are looking for California or west coast authors. Visit their website at www.californiareads.com or contact the California Reading Association's office at 3186 D-1 Airway, Costa Mesa, CA 92626 or (714) 435-1983.

ccpl.carr.lib.md.us/authco/index.htm

The purpose of Mona Kerby's The Author Corner is to create pages that are "clearly written and appropriate for students in grades 2–10." The hope is that you use this site and then "visit libraries, talk to librarians, write to authors, and most especially, read more books." There are links to many author and illustrator websites and a specific listing of mid-Atlantic authors and illustrators (with links to their websites), including Jane Leslie Conly, Mary Downing Hahn, Eileen Spinelli, Jerry Spinelli, Ruth White, and David Wisniewski.

www.childrensauthorsnetwork.com

"The Children's Authors Network (CAN!) is an organization of critically acclaimed children's authors who are devoted to promoting the literacy of children and inspiring their enjoyment of quality books. Through school visits CAN! authors build connections with teachers and students and enrich the curriculum. By sharing their writing and their lives, CAN! authors make reading relevant and important to children." Visit their website or call for a brochure to find out more about this group of west coast authors and illustrators. Authors include Catherine Cowan, Jeri Chase Ferris, Mary Ann Fraser, Evelyn Gallardo, Joan Bransfield Graham, Robin Rector Krupp, Julie Mammano, Michelle Markel, Alexis O'Neill, Joan Prestine, April Halprin Wayland, and Janet Wong. Phone: (310) 545-9582, fax: (310) 545-8218.

www.childrensbookguild.org

The Children's Book Guild of Washington, D.C. is a professional organization of published authors and illustrators, and specialists in children's literature. At their website, visit their Speaker's Bureau, which lists members of the Guild who are willing to book speaking engagements both in their home locations and out of town. Representative titles are listed with each author and illustrator, and each listing includes contact information (website, snail mail, and e-mail addresses), audience, fee, and additional details that will be helpful in learning more about the author and the author's presentation.

www.cynthialeitichsmith.com

Children's book author Cynthia Leitich Smith's website contains a wealth of information about children's literature, including information about authors and illustrators. She also presents information about doing a virtual visit and provides all the information you will need to prepare for a virtual chat. "Children's book authors and illustrators dedicate their voices and visions to bringing art and language to young readers. Many are also fascinating, humorous, inspiring speakers." Information on planning a school visit is included on her site. Authors can be accessed alphabetically by last name, and she has a list devoted to Texas authors and illustrators.

www.co.seminole.fl.us/comsrvs/library/
kids/kids_authors.html

A listing of websites of living and nonliving authors of children's books, sorted by picture books, novels, and nonfiction. Also included at this website are listings of books on a variety of topics.

www.harperchildrens.com/hch/parents/schoolvisits.asp

HarperCollins Children's Books has an author visit section with helpful tips. They update their list of authors and illustrators frequently and suggest you e-mail catherine.balkin@harpercollins.com for a current list. They provide information about organizing an author visit, including specifics for ordering books through them.

www.leeandlow.com/calendar

Multicultural children's book publisher Lee & Low's website has a calendar. Click on the month and find out when your favorite authors and illustrators are touring. You can contact the marketing department through this website for more information. Some of their authors and illustrators include Joseph Bruchac, Pat Mora, Dom Lee, Hector Viveros Lee, Edith Hope Fine, Javatka Steptoe, Matthew Gollub, and many more.

www.mcelmeel.com/writing/page_lin.html

A website for the informative book about author's visits by Sharron L. McElmeel, *ABCs of an Author/Illustrator Visit*. (Worthington, OH: Linworth, 1994.)

magdanz.com/books/river/authors.htm

A page of links to many children's book authors and illustrators who make school visits is hosted by author Jim Magdanz. All authors listed on this site have e-mail capabilities, making contacting the author easy. The sampling of the authors' titles are listed below their names for quick reference, and by clicking on the name you visit the author's website. There is also a page on FAQs regarding author visits.

members.aol.com/ddpattison/scbwi.html

The Society of Children's Book Writers and Illustrators (SCBWI) of Arkansas has a speaker's guide. Each listing includes contact information, publications, and program topics. Although a small resource, this is a perfect one for those who live in Arkansas. If not, visit the SCBWI website (www.scbwi.org) and see the listings of regions for a similar website of authors and illustrators in your area.

www.randomhouse.com/teachers/kit/index.html

Random House's website presents a list of Random House children's book authors and illustrators who are willing to speak at a school or library or for teachers and adults only. The list of authors/illustrators is alphabetical by last name and includes the geographic location of the person, including some for international authors/illustrators. The list also identifies the appropriate ages of audience members for each presenter. Contact information by phone, fax, and e-mail and specific names of marketing staff are included. Review the list of authors and complete the Request Form, and you're on your way for planning a visit. The website includes helpful information about organizing a visit and specifics about book ordering from Random House.

www.rickwalton.com/bring.htm

Children's book author Rick Walton's website includes a listing of authors who live in Utah and are available to visit your school. To learn more about them, click on their names and read their contact information, presentation topics, prices, and a bibliography of their work. An especially helpful source if you live in the Utah area.

www.scbwi.org/member.htm

This is the section of web links to the personal websites of some members of the Society of Children's Book Writers and Illustrators. Names are listed alphabetically by last name. Click on a letter for the author's last name, or browse the entire list to search for your author. A helpful resource. There is also a listing of regions with contact information regarding authors and illustrators in the states or regions.

www.scbwinorca.org/authors_%26_illustrators.html

This site provides a listing of authors and illustrators who live in northern California. It identifies where each author lives (city and county) and links to authors' websites. A valuable tool if you are looking for someone near the northern California area.

teacher.scholastic.com/authorsandbooks/ authorvisit/overview.htm

This website, prepared by Scholastic, Inc., will assist you in contacting Scholastic authors. You can complete an Author Visit Request Form and submit it to Scholastic. The form will provide them with all of the information they will need to handle your request. They list authors who are interested in visiting schools by state; their listings even include Venezuela. Click on the author's name, and you will find out more information about the author and his or her books.

www.scils.rutgers.edu/special/kay/author.html

At Kay E. Vandergrift's website from Rutgers University, there are more than 600 links to author and illustrator sites. The website also identifies biographies and autobiographies about authors, as well as videos that introduce authors and illustrators to their readers. Each video visits a creator of favorite children's books.

www.sdcoe.k12.ca.us/iss/library/authors.htm

A listing of authors and illustrators from San Diego County, their books, and information about preparing for an author visit is located at the San Diego County Office of Education's website. Especially helpful if you live in San Diego or southern California.

www.sharyn.org/

Provides a listing of authors and illustrators from A–I, J–Q, and R–Z. "The authors' homepages are either by the authors themselves, educators/resource collectors, or devoted fans."

www.snowcrest.net/kidpower/authors.html

Here you'll find a listing of children's book authors who enjoy visiting schools, listed alphabetically by last name with representative titles of their work. Click on their names and you'll go to their websites, which will provide more information about their books, presentations, and contact information. An outstanding resource, although I found that some of the websites were no longer correct. There is also a section of FAQs regarding author visits.

www.tonibuzzeo.com

Author and school library media specialist Toni Buzzeo's website links with authors and illustrators who visit schools and also connects with valuable information about making a school or library visit outstanding. Toni (with author Jane Kurtz) is the author of *Terrific Connections with Authors, Illustrators, and Storytellers: Real Space and Virtual Links.* (Englewood, CO: Libraries Unlimited, 1999.)

usawrites4kids.cjb.net/

At this site you can search for information about authors and their books alphabetically or by state. Just click on the state or an alphabet letter to get started, and then visit links to find out about children's book authors. America Writes For Kids! is a project of the Drury University Department of Education, supported by the Springfield-Greene County Libraries and Ozarks Public Television. Its goal is to promote literacy and creativity by introducing young readers, parents, teachers, and librarians to the work of "real, live" children's authors. All children's authors currently living in the United States who have at least one trade book available in the Springfield-Greene County Libraries are invited to join America Writes for Kids! Write to America Writes For Kids! c/o Drury University, 900 North Benton Avenue, Springfield, MO 65802, e-mail: sasher@lib.drury.edu.

www.waterboro.lib.me.us

The Waterboro Public Library has an alphabetical listing of all authors who live in Maine and identifies the children's book authors.

Index

About the Author

Helen Foster James has more than twenty years' experience working in education as a classroom teacher, media specialist, and coordinator of library media services. She currently teaches children's literature at San Diego State University. She has a background in curriculum and instruction and received her doctorate from Northern Arizona University.

She reviews children's books for *School Library Journal* and has contributed articles to various other journals, including an article (February/March 2002) entitled "Bullies and Bullying" for *Book Links*. She has a regular column in *The California Reader*, the California Reading Association's journal. A former member of the California Young Reader Medal committee and the International Reading Association's book award committee, she currently serves as a judge for the National Parenting Publications Awards for Children's Books.

Although passionate about children's literature, she also enjoys camping and hiking in the Sierra Nevada Mountains, traveling, and spending time with friends and family.